Alanna
So glad our
paths are cr
again — J

MW01093232

Twin Rivers

*Joy and sorrow are twin rivers
running through the terrain of life.*

Joyce A. Johannesen

Joyce A. Johannesen

EPH 3:20-21

Ideas into Books® W E S T V I E W
Kingston Springs, Tennessee

Ideas into Books®
W E S T V I E W
P.O. Box 605
Kingston Springs, TN 37082
www.publishedbywestview.com

Copyright © 2023 Joyce A. Johannesen
All rights reserved, including the right to reproduction, storage, transmittal, or retrieval, in whole or in part in any form.

ISBN 978-1-62880-282-5

First edition, November 2023

Cover Photo: Joyce A. Johannesen; Back Cover Author Photo: Roxanna Isabel Roman

Good faith efforts have been made to trace copyrights on materials included in this publication. If any copyrighted material has been included without permission and due acknowledgment, proper credit will be inserted in future printings after notice has been received.

Digitally printed on acid free paper.

Questions of the Soul

When your love has been rejected, how do you love?
When your love is never enough, how do you love?
When your love is shattered, how do you love?
When your love is betrayed, how do you love?

When your dreams are but shadows, how do you dream?
When your dreams never come true, how do you dream?
When your dreams are scorned by those you love, how do you dream?
When your dreams turn to nightmares, how do you dream?

When you're misunderstood, how do you understand?
When your understanding is deficient, how do you understand?
When your understanding is false, how do you understand?
When your understanding is clouded by pain, how do you understand?

When no one in your life has ever loved, dreamed, or understood you.
How do you love,
How do you dream,
How do you understand?

You turn to God and pray.
Begging God for love, dreams, and understanding.
And you cry a waterfall of tears.
And sometimes, you wish to die.

ONE

*T*here he was! At my door! A Miracle! After months of aloneness and prayer, there he stood.

God answers prayer! Allen, the prodigal husband had returned. Just like a Biblical story, the wanderer was looking for grace. He had bowed his knee in the middle of a ballfield and asked God to forgive him. God had, he said. God does those things.

Our two sons, Nicholas and Justin, were living with me in a nice apartment. Nicholas was about to start kindergarten and Justin was still working on potty training. The freezer held "Andes Candies" and a successful trip to the toilet would be rewarded with this minty green chocolate confection.

The boy I married at the age of 16 was not the man I divorced. He was now a self-righteous and holy man who had multiple affairs, abused me, and abused our children. But here he was, my ex-husband speaking of grace. Wasn't this for which I had prayed? It was the right thing to do. God can restore any marriage. Pray child, pray! And here was the miracle. Hallelujah!

"I'm sorry. I need to go back to Illinois and quit my job. But first, let's get married."

My heart fluttered! God was good. God had done the impossible.

Yes, God can restore a broken marriage. The pastor pronounced it a miracle and pronounced us, Mr. and Mrs., once again. The Pastor had prayed for this moment and thought it was another miracle story that would be fodder for a sermon. The Labor Day weekend trip to Illinois resulted in another honeymoon pregnancy. A third child would join our family.

Now married again, he moved in with me. Nicholas started kindergarten. Nicholas spent his first day of kindergarten with the principal. Perhaps a forerunner of more to come or a continuation of the same.

Many were the exploits of Nicholas. He had been thrown out of Sunday School because he would climb in the windows and bark like a dog. Nicholas learned quickly that attention comes by acting out.

Filled with tremendous energy and creativity, I feared for him. There were many trips to the ER. Amazingly he lived. Equally amazing, his brother lived the night Nicholas practiced knife throwing at a human target, his brother.

The pause in our marriage required a job, I got one. It also inspired me to take the test for a GED. I passed with a high score. Being a high school dropout, this was quite an accomplishment. I also took an adult education typing class. I had no typewriter to practice on, but I memorized the keyboard and would move my fingers in the air attempting to spell out words.

I went to apply for clerical jobs; they wanted proof I could type. I'd sit down at the typewriter for the typing test. I just wasn't good enough. However, I could file. I spent my days in the bowels of a large insurance company filing thousands of premium slips in hundreds of steel drawers. Like my colleagues, very often the premium slips were dumped in the back of a bottom drawer away from the watchful eye of the supervisor, Patsy and her assistant, Carolyn. They sat and watched me all day. The windowless basement and the twin matrons made me feel like I was in prison.

If I had a sick day coming, I'd take it regardless of need. Once because I had called out too many times, I was called to the supervisor's office, aka, the warden. He was a short balding middle-aged man. His name was Carl Jones. He sat in his glass office. I have no idea what he did other than stare at the girls working in his department. He threatened to fire me if I took off too many more days.

Each morning I would drop off Nicholas and Justin at the babysitter. She was the mother of someone I worked with. She was a large woman who sat on the couch all day. She seemed nice. She was cheap and expected her clients to supplement the fee with food. I'd bring large cans of government juice, milk, and cereal.

She seemed kind. Nicholas started complaining that she didn't feed them. I dismissed it. Nicholas probably was just hungrier and felt he didn't get enough. I had to have this babysitter to go to work. I had already moved three times because I couldn't pay rent.

The other thing I noticed is that Justin, not potty trained, had constant and continual blistery diaper rashes. In the days of cloth diapers, diaper rashes were constant. But these were severe. One day I got sick at work and left early. Justin was soaked in urine and feces. He hadn't had a diaper change all day. I needed another babysitter. I couldn't leave my babies with this woman who would never get off the couch.

Now that my marriage was miraculously restored, I quit my job. I had a husband again. And I was pregnant.

Allen was back, things would change. His drinking had stopped. The abuse hadn't. The air was turning cold. Allen caught Nicholas touching himself as little boys are prone to do. With lightning fury, he grabbed Nicholas and started beating him with a long-handled metal shoehorn. With welts forming on his legs Nicholas was thrown outside, in the cold, to stand on the deck in his *underoos.* That would teach him never to touch himself again!

Knowing that the shoehorn could be used on me next, I still begged for Nicholas to be allowed to come inside from the cold. In the chilly air, he was shivering and crying. Allen relented. I held Nicholas trying to comfort us both.

I had made a mistake. I had let Allen back into our lives. Once again, I had vowed before God. For better or worse, I vowed to be his wife until death we parted. And I was carrying another child.

I prayed. Oh, how I prayed for my marriage to be "restored." I had dreamed of the day we'd be together again. Sometimes prayers should not be answered the way we want. This was one of those prayers. Sometimes dreams should never come true. This was one of those dreams. I thought I'd had a miracle. This miracle, this dream come true was a horrible nightmare unfolding before my eyes.

With another baby on the way, I had to stay. I had no choice. Tears of repentance notwithstanding, Allen was unraveling. We were back where we started. Abuse at home, with a good face on Sunday morning. There was no one I could tell.

The drinking resumed. He'd stay out all night. He was remodeling a trailer for two young coeds. He slept with them both between repairing and painting their walls.

I don't know why I stayed. I supposed it was because I had nowhere to go. There were no domestic violence shelters in 1974. No one ever talked about such things. And I still believed in miracles. I wanted one. I prayed desperately for one. God can do the impossible and transform. I believed that.

It was January 1975. I don't recall the exact day or date. I just remember it was January. It was cold. Allen had come home from an all-night sex orgy with the two college coeds. I was furious. The fury overtook the fear. Or maybe it was pregnancy hormones.

My anger had been encouraged by my mother-in-law who shared her answer to the problem. She told me to meet him at the door with a knife, grab his "thing" and threaten to cut it off. She said she had done that with one of her ex-husbands. She said it worked. But I knew better – the knife might be used on me.

I don't remember much of the fight. I do remember leaving the apartment. Racing down the back-deck stairs to the gravel driveway, I ran to the car. I had the keys.

He came after me. He grabbed the ice scraper out of the car to clean the windows. Nicholas at school, Justin in my arms, I screamed, and cried.

Seeing his anger, now knowing full well that a beating was soon to come, I locked the car doors. Infuriated, he pushed open the small vent window of the car and reached the handle. He was able to open the door.

He beat me. He beat me mercilessly. Then he got in the car driving like a maniac. I pleaded with him to let me out of the car. He did. He stopped at a gas station and said, "get out."

Justin and I got out of the car as the gas station attendant stared in amazement. I wasn't bleeding. He had been careful where and how he hit me. I was crying. A black river of mascara ran down my face. I used a payphone and called my mother.

We never lived together as man and wife again. I returned to that apartment one last time. Taking off the wedding ring that had been consecrated and placed with a promise to never take it off my finger. One last look. I looked at the inside of the ring where we had engraved declarations of love. The ring I wore said, Love Allen. With one deep breath, I threw that ring as far as I could from the second floor back deck. Surprisingly, it landed far away in the field behind the house. I couldn't retrieve it. It was forever gone.

I lost all my belongings other than my precious boys and a few clothes. I abandoned the apartment I could no longer afford. With those belongings were my parents' bedroom set that I had inherited from her when she bought her trailer. Now it was to that trailer I moved. I occupied it alone with my boys as I waited for my child to be born. My mother lived with her new husband in his house and the trailer was empty.

I drove a beloved white 1969 Volkswagen Beetle that now bequeathed to me. That bug took us to welfare appointments, prenatal care at the Medical Center, church, and the park. I awaited the next member of our little family.

I no longer begged God for Allen to come back. I did beg God for a daughter. I loved my sons, but I was sure this was my last child. I was an outcast. I believed I was so undesirable that I'd be alone for the rest of my life. Certainly, having a daughter would make it better.

At my next OB appointment, I met my new family practice resident. He would be the one who would perfect his craft with me as his patient. He asked me if I had any unusual circumstances.

I said yes. I hung my head in shame. My husband left me and I'm alone with two kids. His words briefly lifted my shame. He was compassionate and kind. He said, *"I'm going to take good care of you."* He did.

He introduced my case to two women in the practice. A PhD Nurse Practitioner and an MSW. This trinity seemed to believe in me, cared for me, and my family as if we were worthy. I was not familiar with a feeling of worthiness. I still thank God for them.

Two other angels stepped in to help me, Rebekah and David Singleton. I met them at church. They owned a large hog farm. David shared with me one time that being a millionaire was not that impressive. Why? Because he was one.

Allen had worked for the Singletons for a short while. Both were leaders in charismatic ministries. They would pray for you for any need or problem. They'd cast demons out. They also gave me money and meat from their freezer. They had faith and expressed it in tangible ways (James 2:17 NKJV *Thus also faith by itself, if it does not have works, is dead*). Most of all, they knew the greatest commandment is to love.

It was three weeks before my due date. I had a fever. I had some pain. I went to the clinic. None of my support systems were there that day. Another doctor examined me and said I was fine. The fever was due to a Urinary Tract Infection. Antibiotics and rest were prescribed.

Allen's sister Julie had agreed to watch Nicholas and Justin when I went into labor. She agreed to take them for the weekend since I wasn't feeling well. I didn't want to be alone.

I called Rebekah. She said come to our home. I went. After food for my body, and prayer, I went to bed in their son's room. He moved to the basement with the pet raccoon. I tried to sleep.

I was in pain, and it continued and escalated. I remember thrashing on the single bed in the teenage boy's room. Wondering, praying, I was scared as my fever spiked. It was the first time I had a UTI; I had no idea what to expect. The doctor told me I had plenty of time before the baby came.

At 2 a.m. I got up to go to the bathroom. Tiptoeing, I silently slipped into the bathroom. I was bleeding. Dr. Halverson had given me his home telephone number for such an emergency. I called him. I apologized for waking him. He said meet me at the hospital.

I walked to the Singleton's bedroom door and knocked. "Rebekah, can you drive me to the hospital?" Off we went. I had no idea what to expect. I had been told I wasn't in labor. I was told I had plenty of time before the baby would be born.

Rebekah drove a big white Cadillac. As she started the car, she prayed. She prayed in English; she prayed in tongues. She rebuked everything she could think of and prayed for my child.

A black cat also crossed our paths that night. With that she exclaimed, "Oh, did you feel that?" With that she hit the gas, rebuked the devil, and got us to the Medical Center where Dr. Halverson was waiting.

No birthing rooms were available in 1975; it was to a cold exam room I went. I was in labor. It was time for the enema. Everyone in labor in 1975 had to have an enema. Trips to the bathroom while ready to push my child into the world were the unpleasant result. No labor room this time, a swift trip to the delivery room, alone, I was ready to deliver.

Once in the delivery room Dr. Halverson took his place. Inserting his gloved fingers, he said I was fully dilated at ten centimeters. I was ready to push.

I hadn't seen Rebekah since the Emergency Room. I was alone, all alone. I assumed she was somewhere. I was quite sure she was praying. It was a particularly good thing that she was.

Between pushes I wondered and worried. I was worried about our future. I wondered if I could provide for this new child. I breathe another prayer for a girl.

I knew God. I'd known Him since I was a child. I had received Jesus as my savior many times. I was always riddled with guilt over all the sins I committed as a child. I knelt at an altar every time the call was given. One can't be too careful about one's salvation if you are full of guilt. Perhaps God would help me. If not for me, at least for these innocent children.

My life was over. Allen and I had remarried. I had such hope. I thought for sure we were going to be that couple with the great testimony of a marriage restored. He would once again answer the call on his life to ministry. I would be a preacher's wife. I would be respected. But here I was, ready to bring another welfare child into the world.

I had a roof over my head, but it was sparse. I had no job. I had no skills. I lived on welfare, food stamps, and WIC (Special Supplemental Nutrition Program for Women, Infants, and Children). My AFDC (welfare) check was $150 a month. I would get a $20 raise for this next child. In return for this money, I would go every six months to be reevaluated for welfare. It was a demoralizing but necessary experience.

Push. Push. My feet were high in the stirrups. I kept pushing. Masked faces of strangers gave instructions. The baby's heart was being monitored. It stopped. No sound. What's happening?

With lightning reflexes, Dr. Halverson grabbed the forceps. I had no anesthesia, no epidural, nothing. Everything began to blur. With precision, he pulled the baby out of me. It was so quick that I was amazed to see a ball of flesh being whisked across the room by the doctor.

Was that my baby? Was my baby born? There was no cry. The pediatricians attended to the baby. Dr. Halverson began to repair my torn flesh.

I asked him, *"is the baby all right?"* He said, *"I don't know."* Then I said *"what was it? Is it a boy or a girl?"*

His answer terrified me. He said *"I don't know. It was so quick I didn't look. It's not good."*

As he walked over to the warmer where the pediatricians were suctioning and checking vitals, he came back and said, *"It's a girl."*

Delighted all I could think of was, I have a daughter, a daughter… He looked at me again and said, *"don't get too excited, it's not good. I don't think she is going to make it."*

The pain, the noise, the smells of the delivery room all mixed with my emotions. Should I be happy? I had a girl. Should I hold my emotions in fear that she wouldn't live? Would I get to hold her?

I said her name to myself, ***Elizabeth Joy***.

Before taking her to the ICU, they quickly showed her to me. No touching. No breastfeeding right after birth. Just a quick glimpse of my daughter was all I was allowed. I was very alone and very terrified.

Once in the recovery room, they inserted a catheter. I was told not to get out of bed. Three other women were sleeping after the delivery of healthy babies. Then Rebekah appeared.

I was so glad to see her. If there was any hope for my daughter's life, I thought her prayers would do it. She smiled. I whispered, *"it's a girl."* The *Glory Hallelujahs* loudly rolled out of her mouth. Tongues followed. The nurse came in and told us to be quiet.

I said *"Rebekah, it's not good."* She said, *"God is able."* I clung to that.

In the morning they took me to a private room. This was a luxury never given to a woman on welfare. They said it was because of the fever and UTI. The truth was, they feared Elizabeth would die. They didn't want me in a room with other women as they held and caressed their newborn babies. Still tethered to an IV pole, I went to the sink and washed my hair. Rebekah went home to get some sleep. I was all alone in a spacious room with big windows.

Elizabeth had aspirated just before she was born. She was born with pneumonia. She was three weeks early. Small but over 5 lbs. she laid in the Isolette in the same hospital as her brother had six years before.

It was a beautiful Saturday morning. Dragging the IV pole, I walked over to the window. A sea of caps and gowns streamed out of the Hearnes Center. It was commencement at the University of Missouri.

Commencement is a funny word; it means a beginning and yet it is a culmination and recognition of an accomplishment. My peers, some I went to High School with, were launching into the world armed with an education and self-respect. I had none of this. I was on welfare. I was a single mom of three. Single motherhood was rare at the time. Or would I be the mother of two and bury a daughter?

Allen was nowhere to be found. Neither was my mother. I was alone. I was a failure. I had always been a failure.

Tears streamed down my face. There was no future for me. I cried and cried. I wondered and worried about the future. As I looked at the graduates, a voice I believe was God spoke to my spirit. It said, "You don't know if you don't try." Could I try? Try what? What would become of us? How did I get here?

TWO

I am a mistake. Yes, I was a mistake. Like millions of children, I was not planned or wanted. I like to think that on some level, at least at times, I was valued. And even loved. But I was never wanted.

How do I know? I was told.

"Mommy, what was it like when you found out you were going to have a baby?" Yes, I remember asking that question many times. Perhaps I thought the answer would change. It didn't.

Unlike other unplanned children – the other oops – my mother never sugarcoated it and said: *"oh, I was so surprised."* Like when you get a gift you didn't expect.

No, she preferred reality. *"We didn't want to have any more children and I didn't know how your dad would feel."* How would my dad feel? What did she mean?

Being a bit precocious, I would ask those questions. Her answer was equally stark, *"Your dad was so old. I don't think he wanted more children."*

I don't remember ever asking her *"did you?"* I knew. She didn't want more children. She had her perfect blonde-haired blue eyed firstborn. He was the most beautiful child ever born and smarter than anyone else would ever be. And she had a second son. I don't think being second was any better than being third. I do think being a girl may have been a slight edge. She clearly only wanted one perfect child and she had already had him.

Before Elizabeth was born, my mother told me to have an abortion. *"Put your sons in foster care, abort your baby, and get your life together."* I've wondered if she ever visited a seedy location to terminate a pregnancy. Unlike other evangelicals, she supported abortion until she realized that this would be a litmus test of faith. She would also tell me that her mother, who gave birth to ten children, had other children who slipped into eternity as victims of a self-performed abortion with a clothes hanger. She would say, "I don't blame Mum. She had so many children."

I was a mistake. How could I prove I belonged in this world? Church, God, Jesus, perfect behavior – this was the ticket. My mother made me memorize lots of scripture and new Sunday School songs so I could be the demonstration model to my peers. This did serve me well. Not just for attention and approval and some love, but for public speaking skills. I've never been afraid to get up in front of people and talk.

There were some good times. They came if I behaved very well or learned the scripture or the song. The process of learning new songs sparks a fond memory. We'd sit at the large upright piano. My mother played the melody and chords, and we'd sing together. We'd sing through the Sunday School music book. We'd sing through the hymnal.

When she'd pick a selection for the Easter program, or the Christmas program, or other special events, I was prepped to be the star. I was like the gold star on a chart. The more stars I earned, the more love she gave. I needed lots of stars since I was a mistake. It was in my hands to prove my worth.

There were also wooden spoons, and a hairbrush broke over my bare backside. There were odd things like having to assist her by washing her back while she enjoyed her Saturday night bath. Seeing her naked was unsettling. She prepared me for my period by calling me to the bathroom to retrieve her used sanitary napkins to put in the kitchen trash can. I wondered why we never put a trash can in the bathroom.

There was yelling. There was guilt. There was shame. This meant I needed lots of salvation. I could sing *"Jesus Loves Me."* But I wasn't sure I could earn His love. I don't know who first added a verse to this song. It went *Jesus loves me when I'm good when I do the things I should.* That verse was written for me. I must perform. Love always came after performance. Love was earned. Why would I think Jesus would be any different? Could Jesus love a mistake?

My dad was old. He was in his early 50s when his third and last child was born. I never asked him how he felt when he found out a new baby would come into their family. I honestly do not know what he would say. I do know that he loved me.

I would walk miles with him through the streets of Brooklyn. We walked to the park, to the beach, to the pier, to the ferry, to the subway. Those subway stairs were like the yellow brick road leading to OZ – a trip to the city (Manhattan), to the Bronx Zoo, to a museum, to Liberty Island to climb the spiral stair to the top of Lady Liberty and peer out the windows in the crown.

When I grew breasts, my dad became more distant. Was it just his own aging? Was it his discomfort with a daughter who was becoming a woman? I don't know.

Growing up in Brooklyn in the 1950s and 60s was magical in many ways. My block was a small town. There were lots of interesting people –

Italians, Jews, Catholics, Protestants, Puerto Ricans, etc. It was a working-class neighborhood where we were all equal. All my friends had relatives from "the old country." Most of our social circle, who came from the church, were Norwegian.

I was born on a Thursday evening in early November. My mother walked to the hospital with my father's niece. She was sent back home. A short time later, labor became more active, and the two women walked back to the hospital. My mother says they gave her "twilight sleep" for the pain. The story never included any information about my dad.

Seven weeks later, on a cold Christmas morning, I was brought by parents to Salem Gospel Tabernacle, to be dedicated to the Lord. Being dedicated to Jesus on Christmas makes me think I am bit of a Christmas child.

Our family traditions were all Norwegian. Christmas Eve was the start of Christmas in our Norwegian neighborhood in Brooklyn. We put up our tree and had our presents all on Christmas Eve. We were still singing around the Christmas tree well into January.

Christmas day was for church. We'd dress up in the morning and walk to church. It was just like Sunday minus Sunday School. Sometimes we would crunch in the snow or put on galoshes for the slush of melting snow. There was a holy hush on Christmas morning.

Of course, I remember nothing of my first Christmas. I would beg my mother to tell me the story though; I loved to hear it. It made me feel less unwanted. On my first Christmas, they crunched through snow or slush to worship God, and give thanks for their Savior who was born on Christmas day.

Pastor Arthur Johnson was the pastor at the time. That morning, my parents passed their unwanted and unexpected infant daughter over to him. He prayed. He thanked God for me. He prayed I'd come to know Jesus later in life. He prayed that God would watch over me. Like Hannah dedicated Samuel to the Lord, I was now set apart and dedicated to God on Christmas morning.

Norwegians are quiet. Norwegians are reserved. But we were Norwegian Pentecostals. Pentecostals aren't quiet. Pentecostals aren't reserved. We clapped our hands when we sang. Usually, it was offbeat because Norwegians have little sense of rhythm. They raised their hands in worship but compared to the Italian Pentecostals, we looked more like Lutherans.

I liked my Italian friends. Their families were loud and ate a lot. My best friend's grandmother was from Italy – the delight of a meal at her house was the *coolie* (the end piece) of the loaf of fresh Italian bread. Grandma Rose played ragtime music on the piano. Her body would slide all over the bench as she played. It was happy music.

We played hopscotch. We skated in the street in metal skates that needed a key. We listened for the jingle of the Good Humor man or the music of the Mr. Softee truck. During the 1959 election season, we took free rides for Kennedy. Behind the cab of a truck, was the *Whip*. This was a ride that spun fast on the corners. My parents opposed Kennedy because he was Catholic. I took the rides anyway. And I would yell Nixon as I spun around just to please my mother.

After Kennedy was assassinated Lyndon Johnson drove through our neighborhood several times. I saw him. Touched his limo. The first of several times I've seen a sitting president.

Later he came through the neighborhood with RFK – Bobby. I didn't know they were enemies because they were all smiles. They stopped in front of Our Lady of Perpetual Help, the majestic Basilica in the neighborhood. LBJ and RFK waved and shook hands. I got very close. The Secret Service shooed me away from the car.

Summers were spent at Sunset Park pool. My dad taught me to swim in the pool. I learned to walk quickly through the woman's locker so as not to see the naked woman. There were no private areas, and you weren't allowed to change in the toilet area. I'd come out all smiles, wading through the trough of water, hit the shower, and jump in. A nickel to swim and a nickel for an Ice on the way home.

Other times we went to Coney Island. The waves, the smell of suntan lotion, the sound of a vendor trudging through the sand selling hot knishes, and ice cream sandwiches – all made for a magnificent summer. It didn't bother me that we didn't have a summer place in the Catskills or on Long Island like most of my friends from church. I had the pool and Coney Island.

Coney Island also meant Nathan's frankfurter and crinkled fries in a paper cone. No ketchup on the fries for me. I ate them plain. The *frank* was also plain. When my taste buds matured, my *frank* hid under sauerkraut and brown mustard.

Later, as I learned the subway routes, my cousin and I would venture to Brighton Beach on hot summer days. We changed subways at the Coney Island stop and traveled two more stops. We'd swim and look at the older Jewish woman roasting in the sun at Brighton Beach.

We walked the boardwalk back to Coney Island. We'd look at boys and occasionally flirt. We played a few games of "Skee Ball" if we had enough money. A stop at Nathan's for fries became the exit ritual as we left a day of sun and waves.

My dad was illegal. Or "undocumented" as is now preferred. He came illegally to the United States the same year my mother was born, 1918. He was 19; he was a merchant marine sailing for Norway. I've seen pictures of the ship he sailed on during the *Great War* (World War I). It looked like a pirate ship with billowing white sails. This ship, the *John Lockett*, was built in 1884 by the British. It was purchased by the Norwegians in 1911. It was sunk by the Germans, April 26, 1917. Everyone survived and all were transported to Le Havre France.

I have often wondered about my dad's youth. I know nothing about it. He died when I was 19. There are so many questions I never asked. This leaves me to fantasize and wonder.

In my dad's photo album was a picture of a young woman. I would ask my mother, who is this woman? She could identify all his relatives even though she had only met very few of them. She would scowl and say, "oh that's your father's girlfriend in Norway." I never knew if she was joking or if he had a girlfriend in Norway.

Long after he died, I learned that he had two older sisters living in the New York area when he arrived. Josephine died young in the Spanish Flu epidemic. Sofie returned to Norway. In my childhood, I met Sofie's daughter. Although she was a cousin, I called *Tante* (Norwegian for Aunt). She had children older than me. My dad sponsored her and her family. We seldom saw them.

In addition to the questions about his youth, I know nothing about the nineteen years between his illegal entry and his marriage to my mother. She was 19 years his junior and young enough to have been his daughter. All I know is that he *put up metal ceiling* and had a long scar on his arm from a deep cut from the metal. I don't recall if it was on the same arm as his anchor tattoo; both spoke of a life I knew nothing about.

I have a sepia tone picture of my dad in a very ill-fitting suit with his best friend, a Norwegian man named Jensen. I look at that picture and wonder what his life must have been like. Were there women? My brother insists that's unlikely. But there was that picture saved in the photo album of the Norwegian girlfriend.

I also have some black & white photos of my parents around the time they married. My mother was very stylish and my father quite handsome. Her clothes belied her humble background and meager employment. His suit fit. They looked like they might have loved each other. But by the time I was born, I saw no romance. Just the grind of daily life and counting out pennies to survive.

My mother was working as a domestic when they met. She was born in a small town in Pennsylvania. One of ten children, she only knew poverty. At 16 she gave up education for the adventure of moving to Brooklyn NY to work for a Jewish family in Flatbush. She would cook and clean in return for a small salary, and room and board. She would talk about the experience almost wistfully. My mother always admired people who had money.

Where did a girl from tiny Waynesboro PA and a man from Arendal Norway meet in Brooklyn? At church! A Pentecostal church pastored by the same pastor who led her first to faith in Waynesboro Pennsylvania.

St.ly Brother Bender married my parents in December of 1938 in a double wedding with another couple. The other couple were Italian. I suppose they were all trying to save money. When asked about their wedding, all my mother would say is that it was a double wedding ceremony and that her father came late, nearly missing the wedding.

I never met any of my grandparents. They were just photos on my parent's respective bureaus and random stories. I was frightened of my Norwegian grandmother Sigrid "Siri" Jonsdatter with her tight thin lips, tight bun, and no smile. My grandfather Johannes Jonassen was a robust man. He looked more pleasant.

My mother's father, Grandfather Bertram Bronson Bumbaugh, was reportedly a bit of a grifter. My mother learned long after he had passed that he fathered a child in addition to the ones he had with her mother. I believe it was a boy. Her sister had a copy of the receipt from paying his fine for fathering a "bastard child."

He also attempted suicide. My mother said he was under "conviction" because he didn't know Jesus. He tried to hang himself but was found. I understand he drank a lot. He did eventually find Jesus but his reputation as a grifter continued. He died when I was a baby. He collapsed in an apple orchard while doing farm work. His last residence was a shack in a junk yard.

My grandmother Minnie Gertrude seemed to be a long-suffering individual who died relatively young. She had a stroke and never recovered. Likely, she had little medical care and languished until she passed. My mother would say, "*my poor mum, she had too many children. I don't blame her for getting rid of some of them.*" My mother said she knew there was a set of twins that didn't live.

When I travel near Waynesboro, I often stop and visit my grandparents' graves and pay my respects. Something my mother never did. I imagine I am the only one who ever visits those graves.

My mother was complex. She was not a happy person. I understand why. A childhood filled with trauma always leaves its wounds and vexes a person for the remainder of their life.

THREE

*T*here are no porches in Brooklyn. There are only stoops. They may be wooden or concrete with banisters of wood, rich brownstone, or black wrought iron. They may be three steps or ten. You may be able to slide down the banister. Or you may ride it while pretending to be on the Steeplechase ride at Coney Island, riding the mechanical horse. Or with your cap gun on your hip, you may fantasize about being Annie Oakley or The Lone Ranger riding to save the day.

The stoop is the centerpiece of the airy – or airy-way. The airy might have flowers but usually, it was concrete. My world was concrete. Predictable. Hard but safe.

Concrete is a wonderful thing. You can walk on it. You can skate with metal skates on it. The airy fences hold you up as you learned to skate. You can run on concrete but if you fall, your knees will bear scabs for weeks, scabs with a fading red mercurochrome halo. You could play Mother-May-I or draw Potsy squares (aka hopscotch).

Colored chalk created flowers or white chalk showed the outline of a crime. The sidewalk had rhymes such as careful not to step on a crack and break your mother's back or step on a line, break your mother's spine. Why was it always the mother?

Everything we needed was surrounded by concrete. My life was cemented in church, school, and the neighborhood, Sunset Park. Nothing ever changed. There was a rhythm to life. It was dull. It was black and white with no hints of gray.

Within a half-mile radius was everything we needed. Distance was measured in blocks. The long blocks were about two and a half times longer than the short blocks. Long blocks were between avenues and short blocks ran between streets. I never could figure out if it were twenty short blocks to a mile or if you counted only long blocks.

The subway stop was half of a long block from 434-53rd Street, my earliest home. Four-Thirty-Four was the perfect location. One didn't have to cross the street to get to the entrance to Manhattan, the subway stairs. I loved going down those stairs. Adventures out of the neighborhood started with those steps.

Before the magic staircase was Johnny's, the neighborhood candy store. A fountain area on one side, candy, newspapers, and sundries on the other. The community phone booth was toward the back. The payphone was our family's connection with relatives in Pennsylvania.

Before we had a phone and a phone number, calls were received at Johnny's. There was a call at the candy store. Johnny would disperse someone to our house to alert us to the call. My mother would hurriedly walk the half of a block to ask Johnny for the message. The call were often urgent and signaled an emergency. It was a call to the payphone at Johnny's that told her that her father had died.

At the candy store, she'd return the call dropping many coins into the slot. This allowed three minutes to hear the news. Other times she would initiate a call to alert friends and relatives that she was planning the annual trip to Waynesboro. Even after we got a phone in the house, we still used the public phone for long-distance. If you had an emergency, the police call box was outside Johnny's.

The church was just beyond the subway stop. It was one short block and that half long block. However, you had to cross the avenue to get to the church. You could go down the magic staircase and come up on matching stairs on the other side of the street avoiding the crosswalk, the traffic, or the weather.

Luckily, there was also a candy store across Fourth Avenue if you needed candy to survive through Sunday services. I always did. Sen-Sen breath perfume was necessary for adults. The Sen-Sens masked the pickled herring they had for breakfast.

Next to the candy store was the Norwegian Delicatessen. Nothing was open on Sundays except some candy stores, ice cream parlors, an occasional restaurant, or a Deli. If you lived in Boro Park, the Jewish stores were all open. Most of our neighborhood stores were closed and gated. Nothing was opened on Fifth Avenue except the Norwegian restaurant Promenaden. It was hidden on the second floor.

Halvorsen's, the Norwegian Deli was open on Sundays. If you had unexpected company on Sunday afternoon the deli provided Julekake or Coffee Ring. They also had sliced roasted beef or turkey, Grisle brød, Gjetøst, or Nikkeløst, and potato salad with perfectly sliced potatoes. And just in case you hadn't already bought it, the *Nordisk Tidende*, the Norwegian newspaper was still available.

The bank was a walk of half a long block and one short block. It was on Fifth Avenue. Not to be confused with Fifth Avenue in the "city."

This Fifth Avenue was our Brooklyn shopping mecca. To get to the bank you had to cross the avenue, at the light.

Before the bank, you passed Woolworths. Woolworths was the Wal-Mart of its day. Lined out front, winter, or summer, were the baby carriages. Each pram had a baby in it. The moms would shop inside while their babies napped outside. I would often ask my mother to let me stay outside and look at the babies. At Christmas time, the Salvation Army was stationed outside Woolworths. They rang their bell or occasionally had a live band playing Christmas songs.

The lunch counter had crullers and the sundry counter had curlers. Some of my first cosmetics came from Woolworths. Everything came from Woolworth's or John's Bargain Store. Hardware, clothes, laundry supplies, and bobby pins stacked in bins; lunch or supper could be enjoyed at the lunch counter, or a banana split to cool a summer afternoon. My pets, two birds that I named Petey (they were parakeets) and an assortment of turtles also came from Woolworths.

There was a bargain store that kept changing names, a shoe store, and Lerner's for clothes all in one short block. Access didn't include crossing the street. Cross another one-way street, you could buy fabric for a new dress. Go the other way and get your produce and furniture. Cross at the corner, your meat was secured from the butcher. The more streets you cross, the more important the trip.

The park, beautiful, majestic Sunset Park, was a several block walk. Nevertheless, we went there often. Lots of grass, a pool, a hill for sledding in the winter, swings that went high as you viewed the skyline of the "city" and could wave to Lady Liberty.

Often, I would be pushing my Betsy Wetsy doll in her pram. Betsey came from Albany Store. Albany was a toy store that sold mostly bikes but also had many toys, including dolls. I'd longingly look at all the Ginny dolls in the window. I got my first Betsy McCall doll with bendable legs there. When I bought that doll, it was only time I ever remember going into that store. But I would always stare at the things in the store window when we passed.

Pushing my gray regal-looking pram, I'd stop to check on the "baby" while my dad patiently waited. Other times I just held my dad's hand. As I got older, I would run to the corner and wait for him to guide me safely across the street. Eventually, I just walked by myself.

My dad walked everyday regardless of the weather. On one of those afternoon walks, I went with my dad to the library for the first time. All over the country, there are libraries that were funded by Carnegie.

Massive, impressive buildings can be found in Nebraska or Minnesota that bear the name Carnegie. Our library was a beautiful Carnegie Library.

It had the smell of musty books and wood. We were shhh-ed by the librarian. It was determined I was old enough for my own library card. In a whispered voice, I told her my name and address. I always had to spell my last name. Too many n's and it was SEN, not SON.

We never purchased books. The library was our only source. My dad always bought the *Daily News* but depended on the library to read *The New York Times*. Besides his frugality, it was logistically better to buy the *News* because it was easy to read on the subway. The large newsprint sheets of the *Times* was best read at a table. He was a regular at the library reading the newspaper, but rarely checking out books.

I had my own library card; the maximum number of books were chosen. I always picked the maximum number. I usually didn't read them all. I loved the *Betsy, Tacy, and Tib* series. From the earliest picture books to the early reader books, I followed their stories. I also read some of the *Bobbsey Twins* books.

I graduated to *Nancy Drew*. My friend Karin could read one book in a day and owned them all. I used a bookmark and borrowed them from the library. I remember some of the titles: *The Secret of the Old Clock*, *The Hidden Staircase*, *The Old Attic*. There should have been one about a "Forbidden Door." There wasn't, but there are doors that should be forbidden.

One of my earliest memories is my first walk to Public School 94. I was four. I was ready to enroll in Kindergarten. Neither of my brothers went to Kindergarten. Now it was required. It also required more vaccinations.

My parents believed that public health services were more than adequate. No private doctors for us. The one exception was the private doctor who took out my tonsils in the basement of his office with his wife assisting. Early in the morning, we rode the city bus to the medical block in Bay Ridge Brooklyn. Afterward, I did get ice cream. It was small consolation. A kind neighbor also brought an egg custard for me. I hated it. I was told I was very ungrateful and had to eat it anyway.

Other than my experiences of the tonsillectomy, and later rheumatic fever, everything came from the public health department. I remember standing in a lengthy line at the health center with my father for a polio vaccination. It would be a shot and I couldn't cry because there were too many people in the line.

This time it was my mother who took me to get a vaccination from the school nurse at PS94. I don't remember the shot or the nurse. I do remember the big metal door of the side entrance. Everything seemed so big. That door was very heavy. It made a loud noise as it closed behind us. That was a good door. I had good teachers there.

To get into our home, you needed to pass through at least three doors. One you opened without a key. The second needed a key. If you didn't have a key, you rang the buzzer. Another buzzer would reply which indicated that the lock was released. You were now "buzzed" in to decide between three doors and a staircase. Which way to go?

Two went to our apartment in this three-family house. The stairs went to either the Foley's on the second floor or the Gorman's on the third. I never went up there. And then there was the door to the stairs to the basement. It was under the stairs in a dark alcove. I only went to the basement if I went with my dad. I would run past that door as I walked through the public hallway alone. It scared me. Some doors are scary.

Doors are portals. Most lead to something new, necessary, and often good. Others are not so good. Some should be locked. Some should be forbidden. I was about to go through a forbidden door.

I was told not to talk to strangers, never accept candy from them, or go anywhere with them. I was always an obedient child. Remember, I was a mistake. I had to earn my right to be in the world. Being good was necessary.

Mr. Thompsen was not a stranger. Living near our church and being Norwegian, my father knew him superficially. He introduced me to him one day while my father was cleaning the church.

Mr. Rogers wasn't on TV when I was a child. Later, Mr. Rogers would remind me of Mr. Thompson. He was soft-spoken, seemed kind, and generous. Unlike Mr. Rogers, who loved children, Mr. Thompson loved little girls. I was being groomed.

My face lit up when I saw Mr. Thompsen. He seemed to stand around Johnny's candy store a lot. A fresh coin for a Hershey bar would be my reward for a smile. In the most gentle and kindest of voice, he'd ask me what kind of candy I wanted. As I selected my treat, Mr. Thompsen would stand with his arm on my shoulder. I could have anything I wanted. Sometimes he bought me two.

My parents knew that Mr. Thompsen bought me candy. No one ever questioned. Naively, it was assumed he was just a man who had no children but liked them. Sometimes I would jealously eye him with an arm around another girl offering her candy as well.

I remember him as tall. He had a Norwegian accent, as did almost every adult in my life. He would somehow mysteriously appear at times.

Because of the candy reward, I thought I was blessed. Mr. Thompsen had a beard. He also wore a belt with a big T on it for Thompsen. Seems I was eye level with that belt buckle; it's the thing I remember most about him.

It was chilly. There was a nip in the air, it was Autumn. I was eight. It was a Friday. I know that because later that evening my mother and I walked up the block to Fifth Avenue to shop. Stores were not open in the evening, except on Friday.

I had just finished spaghetti with the coolie of the Italian bread at Barbara's. Grandma Rose played some ragtime for us. The piano was so important it had a room to itself. The houses between her house and mine were few. I didn't have to cross the street. I could stay late.

It was dark when I left 410-53rd Street to walk the few steps to 434-53rd Street. As I shut the outer door to Barbara's house, I saw him. Mr. Thompsen. Would it mean candy?

I had never seen him at night. He was waiting at the bottom of the stoop. Just standing there waiting, smiling. I was delighted because I knew a trip a few steps in the other direction would mean candy from Johnny's.

Mr. Thompsen was about to open a forbidden door. A door I didn't know how to walk through. A door that changes you forever. A door that opens to shame and pain.

Mr. Thompsen said, "*Yoyce, I have something to show you.*" I thought perhaps he had remembered what type of candy I liked and had already bought it for me. Maybe he had a gift for me. I went with him to the dark entryway of a closed business.

He asked me to kiss him. That seemed an adequate price for all the candy he'd given me. My father never allowed me to kiss him on the mouth. It was not fitting for a grown man to kiss a girl on the mouth, even her father. Mr. Thompsen asked me to kiss him on the mouth. I did.

That led to his opening his pants, exposing himself. He pushed my head down gently and said, "lick it like a lollipop." He held my head in place until he released. I vomited on his shoes.

Scared, shocked, I apologized profusely for vomiting. I bent down to wipe his shoes. He told me I'd be a good wife someday. I did very well. We'd practice my being a good wife again. "*You'd like to be a good wife, wouldn't you?*" I would.

Since I had done so well, he said he had a special treat for me. He said it was better than candy. Slipping his hands now in my pants, he opened doors forbidden to children.

I don't remember if we practiced more. I suspect we did. Nevertheless, that is the only time I remember clearly. I walked to my house a different girl. He called to me and said "*remember, this is our secret. Don't tell anyone. You're special.*"

It took less than a minute to walk from Barbara's house to mine. I wonder what went through my mind as I did. Being 8 years old, I am sure it can only be described as confusion.

Too young to understand shame, still I knew something was wrong. I kissed him on the mouth when I knew better. Yet, I always wanted to be a good wife and mother. I dreamed about the day I'd have real babies instead of dolls. Was this what I needed to know to secure my future? Being a mistake, my future was always in question.

We had a bad neighborhood on our block. A small row of houses that my mother called *the tenements*. I wasn't allowed to play with the children who lived there. They might have lice or other diseases. How fitting that I remember being in front of the "tenements" when I told my mother that I had done something bad. I had kissed Mr. Thompsen on the mouth. I felt better that I had confessed. My mother determined to find out more.

Many, many years later, in the only adult conversation with my mother about Mr. Thompsen, she said she was bathing me the next day. Saturday night was bath night. Every other day you washed in the sink. Saturday meant time in the tub and shampoo to get ready for church the next day. It also meant it was time for me to wash my mother's back.

During this bath, she said I told her what else had happened with Mr. Thompsen. Exactly what I told, or even how much, I don't remember. We never spoke of details again. One shouldn't talk about forbidden things and those who passed through its door.

Alarmed, she told my dad. More alarmed, my dad told our Pastor at church the next day. Kindly white-haired Pastor Arne Dahl, the spiritual leader of our world, now knew I had kissed Mr. Thompsen on the mouth and worse.

Always concerned about what people thought, my mother was quite furious that my father had told our Pastor. So often I would hear, "what will the people in the church think?" Why my dad told, I don't know. Now I thank God that he told. But at the time, I thought my mother was right. I had done something bad, something I instinctively knew was shameful. What would Pastor Dahl think of me now?

I clearly remember my mother's anger at the secret being told. Pastor Dahl, wise beyond the experience of his generation called the local police precinct and reported it. Long before mandatory reporting and after school specials on child sexual abuse, Pastor Dahl called the police.

Reports were taken from my parents. My mother was mortified. Two male detectives were put in charge of the investigation. There were no females working a Sexual Victims Unit at the time. No recommendations for therapy. No social workers. Just two middle aged male detectives were working this case.

My mother told me that the police knew. I was terrified. Now all the important people in my life knew what I had done. I also knew this was the end of the candy store trips. I was no longer special and would probably never be a good wife.

The police came to school early that week. Standing in front of my classroom were two detectives and my mother. I was dismissed from school early. My classmates were stunned. My teacher, Miss O'Shea, was nervous.

I went with them to their car. We didn't own a car so being in a car was always an adventure for me. Being in a car meant someone in our church was giving us a ride to a church event out of the neighborhood. Usually, it was a trip to a park or camp. It might mean we were going to the Catskills. It was always fun to be in the back seat of those large cars of the '50s. Not this time though.

The detectives explained to me that they thought they had found Mr. Thompsen. They said they needed me to identify him. That made me feel important and confused. I had betrayed the person who was going to assure me that I would be a great wife. He had told me not to tell. I had told.

In front of the side gate of our church, I sat in the back seat of the car. There were three people by the name of Thompsen living on that block. They had ruled out two. They asked me to stay in the car and watch as they asked the suspected Thompsen to come out on the stoop. I had to turn around to look out the back window of their unmarked sedan.

"Look closely and tell us if this is Mr. Thompson." They were sure they had their man. He was the right age and met the description in every way.

Out came Mr. Thompsen. This Mr. Thompsen had no beard. This Mr. Thompsen was clean shaved. I couldn't say for sure if he was the right Mr. Thompsen. I was told I had to tell the truth. The truth was, I didn't know. The police drove us home.

My mother, still furious about the situation, told me that this too was my father's fault. She said my father had seen Mr. Thompsen while on one of his daily walks. He confronted his daughter's abuser. He told him the police were coming to get him. I had told. He would be arrested. Smart Mr. Thompsen went home and shaved.

I saw Mr. Thompsen around the neighborhood after that. I never was given candy again. I would watch as other girls were brought to the candy store with Mr. Thompsen's arms around their shoulders. I would wonder if they too would be taken to a hallway or his apartment. I had once been invited to his apartment as well. I also regretted that I was no longer special and could have someone buy me any candy I wanted.

Several months later the police came again. This time they had a plan. This time they asked me to talk to Mr. Thompsen when I would see him in the neighborhood. They asked me to tell him I wanted to go to his apartment as he had asked. I did as told.

This is a clear memory. If it weren't, I'd question how it could be true. But I don't question it. I know it is true. I was nine now. I talked to Mr. Thompsen. We agreed that I would meet him in front of my church, by the gate.

The time and place set, I stood in my navy pleated skirt, white shirt and red scarf of school assembly day waiting for my abuser to come. I had been told by the detective to bring library books. It would make it look like I had told my mother that was where I was going.

The detective stood across the avenue and watched. I stood and waited. No one came. It was over. Mr. Thompsen continued to abuse countless girls in my neighborhood luring them with candy. As far as I know, he was never caught.

I was caught. I had walked through a forbidden door. I might never be a good wife!? I was a mistake. I wanted to die.

FOUR

*W*hen you are a kid, everything you think, you experience, you endure, you perceive as normal. You can't compare it because it's all you know. Even if you know someone else does it differently, your family's way must be right, and best.

Same with your thoughts and feelings. It never occurred to me until I had children of my own that it didn't seem that my children wanted to die when they were eight years old, or ten, or twelve or fifteen. I wanted to die at nine and ten. It never seemed odd to me that as a child I thought a lot about dying and wishing to die.

I don't remember saying it aloud. If I did, my mother would have just said something like: *"don't say such a thing."* Often, I would play dead on the floor to see what my mother would do if she thought I was dead.

I also remember trying to hold my breath, so I'd die. Then I learned that you can't do that. Your body will self-preserve, you'll pass out, and start to breathe.

When I'd go to the beach, I'd lament my ability to swim. I wanted to walk into the waves and drown. That would be a respectable way to die. Drowning in the pool would be hard, too many people and too many lifeguards.

When I looked at buildings around me, I wondered how high up was high enough. High enough to hit the ground and die. My eight, nine, and 10-year-old heart thought about this a lot. And it didn't stop.

Somewhere I had heard that killing yourself was murder. I asked my mother about it. Not ever imagining that I would be thinking about suicide, she never thought anything about my questions about death and suicide. She just answered my question. *"**It's murder! You go straight to Hell**."*

I don't believe that anymore. Suicide, while tragic, is a mental health issue. Just like one may die from cancer, a person may die by suicide because of mental illness. It's no different. When I was a kid, it was the biggest of sins, murder.

The though of hell did serve as a deterrent to action but not to thoughts. I had a plan. I remember it. The memory is not clear and sharp. It is like a blurry, faded, black and white picture. The kind where you can't make out who's in it. But if you squint and look at the background you can determine the shadowy figures.

My dad cleaned the church. It supplemented our family income. Money was always tight and carefully rationed. Friday morning breakfast for my parents consisted of counting out his pay, this for groceries, this for the rent, this for the church, this for utilities. My mother didn't work outside the home until later when she became a home caregiver for an elderly rich man. My dad was a janitor who worked nights at a large bank in the *city*.

I would often go with him to clean the church. The church building was built as a house of worship for a Jewish population and later occupied by the Norwegian Pentecostals. It was an old building with lots of secret doors. I would run up and down the back stairs that children weren't allowed to use. I'd open doors that no one used. I liked to explore a balcony no one sat in and a bird's nest baby nursery in the highest rafters. If I were lucky, I could convince a parent to let me watch their baby in that nursery on a Sunday morning.

When my father wasn't looking, I explored the men's room. I was fascinated with the urinal. I'd seen men peeing on the street up against a building. Urinals stink. The urine smell mixed with deodorizing pads was overpowering. I'd never seen or smelled anything like it. I had no desire to ever see it again.

One day, I found the baptistry. In the back of the platform, under the choir area, and under the gold Gothic stenciled giant JESUS sign, there was a door that went to the baptistry. I crawled behind and under it exploring this hidden space.

That was it! This was the plan. I hadn't been baptized yet. I wasn't old enough. But wasn't this a holy place? If I got behind the baptistry and covered myself with a blanket, I could die in a holy place. Seemed this might be the way to escape hell.

My parents would find me and think it an accident. How does a nine-year-old think of such things? I wondered if they'd cry.

I climbed into the baptistry from the back. I held my breath. I covered myself. The walls closed in on me. I couldn't breathe. I coughed. I gasped. It wasn't working. My first attempt at suicide was a failure.

There were other attempts. Childish ones, but real. I would go into the water and try to forget to swim. I always remembered just in time. I'd go underwater, try to breathe in, letting the water take over. I always closed my mouth in time and emerged from the water. No one knew. Just childish stuff.

I'd tried to be good, but I was always sinning. I'd pray to God with fervor, begging Him to forgive me. I'd contemplate if God could tolerate me. Tolerate what? For being.

Of course, there were real sins. I would play cards. Those devil cards, associated with gambling, were strictly forbidden. Barbara's family was Catholic, and they gambled in church. Card games were played regularly. Same with Denise, they were Methodist. Her dad would sit for hours behind a TV tray playing solitaire and smoking. None of them were "saved" because if they were, they wouldn't smoke, play cards, go to the movies, wear make-up, or dance. My duty was to be a good Christian witness, they needed Jesus.

I'd try to convince my friends to play board games like Life, Parcheesi, Sorry, Checkers or Monopoly so I wouldn't sin. Instead, Slap Jack usually won. I learned to break the deck of demon cards, and shuffle. I learned to deal. Then I advanced to Go-Fish and War. Eventually, I learned to play rummy. When my mother would ask me, "Were you playing cards at Denise's house?" I'd lie and say, "*no*."

I don't know which sin was worse, the cards or the lie? Probably the lie because my mother would say often: "*There is nothing I hate more than a liar.*" Hate is a strong word and her tone resounded in my ears.

Or she'd quote the scripture: "*and all liars shall have their part in the lake which burneth with fire and brimstone: which is the second death*" (Revelation 21:8 KJV). I was going to hell for sure. Next time they asked me if I wanted to invite Jesus in my heart, I said yes. Until then I'd lay in bed thinking about hell.

Going to a theater to see a movie was a major sin. I was seven and wanted to go to the movies and see Disney's *Sleeping Beauty*. Everyone did. Barbara went. Denise went. Everyone at school went. Everyone but me. I was a Christian. We didn't do that. What if Jesus came when I was at the movies? What if someone from the church saw me?

I cherished my *Sleeping Beauty* coloring book. I'd pick up my crayons and color Flora, Fauna, and Merriweather. Since I hadn't seen the movie, I couldn't keep them straight. My creation had the fairies wearing the wrong color dress. Everyone laughed at me.

If you wore make-up, you were like Jezebel in the Bible. No one wanted to be Jezebel. Her name was synonymous with evil. But I became a Jezebel in the third grade, and I ruined my Christian testimony. It was May Day. We had prepared a folk dance to be done in the concrete schoolyard. I had a vest and flowers in my hair. Days like that are special.

Surprisingly, they let me dance in elementary school. In Junior High, a note was procured from the pastor stating the sinfulness of dancing in gym class. It was against our religion. Once again, sin overtook me. By ninth grade, I had figured out to not tell my mother we were dancing. No note from the pastor meant I could sin by doing folk dances with other girls in the gym.

But this was third grade. I have pictures from that day. The boy I was dancing with was cute. I probably had a crush on him. I looked through the gaggle of mothers. There she was with her dark sunglasses and hands on her hips. All the mothers were smiling and waving, but not mine.

She only scowled; her lips pursed. Why? What did I do? I didn't know. A black and white photo captures the puzzled deflated look on my face. Then I knew, it was lipstick! I had lipstick on. Sweet and pretty Miss Kathleen O'Shea, my third-grade teacher, called all the girls to her desk and made us beautiful with lipstick.

I hesitated when it was my turn. I knew that it was a sin to wear make-up. I had enough sins in the third grade. It was the same year as Mr. Thompson. She gently summoned me and before I knew it, I was painted. I never could figure out how she could be so nice and yet be such a terrible sinner with lipstick. Now I had sinned.

When I got outside to perform, I had forgotten about the sin. My mother saw it. She never smiled. There were no kind words; there was only condemnation. The walk home was hard. I was told I had ruined my Christian testimony. Not only had I sinned but I had brought shame to myself.

Life changed. We moved twice. New school, a horrible teacher, and finally off to Pershing Junior High School. It was the best school. I loved going to Junior High. It was a fifteen-minute walk to its hallowed halls. I had a bus pass, but I usually walked with girls I knew from PS 94.

We would look at boys and talked about homework. We joked about some of our teachers and complained about others. Overall, we had good teachers. Our friends were diverse, Jewish, Italian, Irish, Protestant, Catholic, Buddhist, Puerto Rican, and African Americans who were bused in from Red Hook. We even had a black teacher, Miss Hopson. She was the Home Economics teacher and she taught me to sew and to make cookies. On the last day of school, I hugged and kissed her on the cheek. I went home thinking that was the first time I touched a black person.

There were plenty of blonde-haired blue-eyed Norwegians. My hair was turning dark like my mother's. I have brown eyes. By ninth grade, I had a Puerto Rican boyfriend. The boyfriend picked me because he thought I was a nice Christian girl. Instead, we kissed a lot after church.

Barbara moved away. Denise was older and didn't live across the street anymore. But I didn't lack for friends. I'd "hang-out" at an ice cream parlor or candy store. My cousin Gladys became my best friend and shadow. We decided to smoke.

Friday was the time for our great cigarette adventure. I'd leave my house on a Friday night right after supper. Walk the seven short blocks to Gladys's house. Off we'd go. Stuffing bottles of perfume in our pockets, we were ready for the evening.

First stop, the candy store to buy a pack of cigarettes, minty gum, and mints. Like everyone, we started with Marlboros. Lured with the rebellious line "*I'd rather fight than switch*" we smoked charcoal filtered Tareyton cigarettes.

Having no place to hide our cigarettes, we had to smoke the whole pack in two hours. Puff, puff, cough, cough – spray perfume. Repeat. Puff, puff, cough, cough. Chew gum. Eat a mint. Repeat.

Cigarette after cigarette, ten each, in two hours meant a new cigarette every twelve minutes. We reeked of nicotine and cheap perfume. Her mother knew and would just laugh. My mother knew and yelled.

"*You've been smoking!*"

"*No, I haven't*" (lie number one).

"*Was Gladys smoking!?*"

"*Of course not, why would you say that?*" (lie number two).

"*Why do you smell of cigarettes?*" She always sniffed my hair and then my breath when she asked this.

"*I was at the ice cream parlor, and everyone was smoking. The smell got on me there*" (lie number two and a half, I had been to the ice cream parlor most of the time and it was filled with smokers).

Soon I decided I wanted to smoke on days other than Friday. This meant I needed to have a hiding place. I found one, behind the radiator in the vestibule in our apartment building.

My mother was smart. She started standing at the second-floor landing to watch me go out the door to school. We lived on a corner, so it was a long block first. I'd look back. She now leaned out of the window to watch.

A quick walk around the block, or a quick backtrack once she went inside, I'd enter the hallway to retrieve the cigarettes from behind the radiator. I never smoked until I was far away from the window. While I puffed, I slipped earrings on my ears and applied some make-up.

Thankfully, I never learned to inhale, and I remembered to take the earrings off before I returned.

I also needed deliverance from the sin of make-up. Along with some pale pink lipstick I bought from a vending machine at a subway stop, the red Maybelline eyebrow pencil was under my underwear in my top bureau drawer. One day upon returning from school, it was waved in front of me and loudly snapped in two. I was going to hell. I bought a new one and hid it with cigarettes.

No doubt about it! I was a sinner. Since suicide wasn't working out for me, I started thinking about running away. My brother had. It was almost like my parents were proud of him. I heard the narrative as if it was from Luke 15, the story of the prodigal son. My brother was the prodigal. He wandered far away from Brooklyn to Arizona. He came to his senses and came home to his natural parents and home to His Heavenly Father. He had left home at 14 and came back at 15. He amazingly was still able to graduate from high school at 16. After high school he went immediately to Bible School to become a preacher. Glory Hallelujah.

A few years later he and his Chinese girlfriend were having a baby and his unrepentant sin got him excommunicated from the church. He was able to repent publicly, and he and his wife were then welcomed into the fold. The golden child always did the right thing eventually. His sins were understandable. His sins were repent-able and forgivable.

But I was a sinner. No matter how much I prayed, I was a sinner. I guess you can't expect much else from a mistake. My brother was the chosen child. The wanted one. Not an "oops."

There were a few church people who tried to reach out to me. Most used guilt but there were a few that loved me just the way I was. I wanted attention. I needed attention. If I couldn't get it being good, maybe I could be the rebel that would be redeemed and have a wonderful testimony. That might do it.

Maybe I could run away and return. Maybe I could use drugs and get forgiven and clean. Maybe I could have sex. Or maybe I'd just be a garden variety sinner who played cards, wore makeup, and puffed on Tareytons.

Could I ever repent enough and find forgiveness? How bad did the sins have to be to have a great testimony and be accepted? Being good and holy was no longer an option. I'd been sinning too much. I needed a big sin and a big repentance.

Thoughts of dying were always lurking in the background. During those Junior High years, we lived in an apartment building with five floors. The staircase ended with a door to the roof. I would go to the roof and peer over the side. I didn't fear dying. I wanted to die. If I jumped off the roof, would I die? Or would I be left paralyzed? It wasn't high enough. I didn't want to be paralyzed so I decided not to jump.

I thought all this quite normal. I thought everyone must be like this. I never thought it had anything to do with Mr. Thompsen. It was that I was a mistake. I was unwanted. Seeds of rejection and shame bloomed into suicidal thoughts that would plague me all my life.

My days at Pershing Junior High were over. Friends dispersed to different high schools. I went downtown to a school in a very tough neighborhood. Wonderful opportunity for more mischief and sinning. To get out of the house, I found some sort of "church" activity every night of the week. I thought increasingly about running away or committing bigger sins.

Like the plan to end my life in the church baptistry, my plan to run-away was doomed to failure. I was chicken. I couldn't do much right, even sinning. But making plans that would fail, I was good at failing. I met a boy at camp. I loved going to camp.

My first experience at camp came when my mother was a counselor and I a very young camper. Our church fellowship rented a camp in the Catskills. Swimming, games, and lots of Jesus, church camp always has lots of Jesus. I also got lice.

Then I went to Ashford Hills, the Salvation Army Sunbeam camp. Captain Johnson took us in a van and said good-bye. Funny, I don't remember any of the children who were on the van with me. Cabin assignment completed, I found myself on an old army cot complete with a scratchy army blanket. This army blanket had probably seen a lot of battles. Emblazoned on the front was the familiar shield of the Salvation Army, God's Army – soldiers of the blood and fire. I was instructed on the art of making my bed with hospital corners. To pass the daily morning inspection the corners must be tight and uniform.

The morning and evening meant chapel. The morning sharpened our Bible knowledge. The evening was come to Jesus time. And of course, we also had quiet time every morning. My personal devotions meant my Bible would be open, and I'd read a verse or two. I'd fold my hands and pray. I don't remember coming to Jesus that year. It a delightful time of Bible, swimming, trees, clean air, and sweet memories.

As I got older, camp meant meeting boys. But before that, I needed to learn a bit about facts of life. My last year at children's camp came with a rude awakening. I had two roommates in a dorm-type room on the second floor near the bathrooms. At night, we would chat.

I suppose we should have been talking about Jesus or something wholesome. But we were adolescent girls and the topic turned to sex and where babies come from. I remember lying on the bunk listening. Elaine declared that you had to have sex to have a baby. I knew what sex was – well, sort of. I watched an episode on Dr. Kildare about teenage pregnancy.

My mother had said how horrible sex and pregnancy outside of marriage were. I was sure my parents could never have engaged in such a horrible activity. I corrected my friend by saying, "NO, Christians don't have sex. God gives them their babies."

They laughed and corrected me. I maintained my position. "Maybe when Christians kiss something happens, and God gives them a baby when they are ready."

A girl, six years my senior, had heard me. One night she came to me while I was crying over some minor offense. She used that opportunity to explain to me that yes, my parents had sex, or I wouldn't be here. Yes, Christians have sex. It's normal. She didn't make me feel stupid. She was gentle and kind. Next year there would be a special boy.

Charlie asked me to be his date for the camp banquet. As I recall, I caught Charlie's eye before he caught mine. Holding hands, we'd wander to the far corner of the campgrounds. In a field far from the buildings of the camp was a wild strawberry patch. Wild strawberry tasting gave way to the sweet taste of a first kiss.

After tearful goodbyes, we vowed to see each other again. There would be "youth rallies" and letters. Phone calling between Long Island and Brooklyn was expensive. We planned and met at the New York City World's Fair for a full day of imagining the "world tomorrow," food, fun, and an occasional kiss. Occasionally we'd run into his mother and younger sister who never liked me and just scowled. I ran into Charlie many years later. He was married to a childhood friend and worked for NYC Sanitation. They later divorced, he remarried, retired to Florida, and died relatively young.

Our last kiss was on a snowy day in December. The excitement of Christmas was in the air. He had come to my neighborhood with a present for me. I quickly went to a store and bought a black turtleneck sweater for him. I don't remember what he gave me. I had not expected a visit or a gift. It was over. The first blush of love is never easy. Like the wild strawberry, its season is brief.

There were some other boys. Most connected with a church or camp. Next was Phil and a trip to PA in the snow. He was dark and Italian. I was attracted to Italian and Puerto Rican boys. On the way home, the bus broke down. When we arrived in front of his church, there was my mother. My face was smeared with mascara from hours of sleeping on a rickety school bus. This time I didn't just ruin my Christian testimony, I was now just doomed for hell's fire. I had applied this make-up all by myself.

There was a guy on the Fifth Avenue bus who is nameless. He showed up a few other places and we would make out. I made up a story about him to my youth pastor. I told Brother Jim and his wife I'd lost my virginity with him. It made them cry for my soul. I think back of Sister Rosemary's tear dropping on my face as they prayed. None of it was true. Many years later I contacted Brother Jim and Sister Rosemary, confessed my lie and asked for forgiveness.

And then there was John with the Polish last name. John was a camper at a camp far in the Adirondacks. For a girl from Brooklyn, being on the Island to meet Jesus in the Adirondacks was an extravagant experience. Jack Wyrtzen's Word of Life Camp attracted campers who were affluent. The camp was expensive. Campers came from private schools in Connecticut or upstate. I was bequeathed a week at camp from the rich woman whose husband my mother cared for – they were *old money* and had lots of it. Thanks to her generosity we benefitted with tickets to the opera, and the ballet.

John was from Connecticut. Bridgeport to be exact. He wasn't affluent. There probably was some kissing and touching in the trees. Nothing serious. By the end of the week, I had another come to Jesus moment and testified around the campfire about how Jesus had saved me (again). But John stayed in my head. We wrote letters. Real letters, the kind that need stamps.

My thoughts turned increasingly to running away. It was time to leave. John never knew about my plan. I planned to go to school with some clothes in my bookbag instead of books. I'd go to the "city" and take the bus to Bridgeport.

I took Trailways or Greyhound to Connecticut often. The younger of my two brothers, his wife, and two daughters lived in Hartford Connecticut. Often, I would take that same route to spend a weekend or a summer week in Connecticut. It would not be difficult to go to Bridgeport.

John would likely help me. I thought it would be good to go somewhere where someone knew me. Who knows, John might even decide he loves me, and we'd be happy ever after. But I had to leave. Somewhere, someone might eventually love me.

I guess I didn't want to go. I self-sabotaged. At church on Sunday night, as the sermon was being preached, I deconstructed an offering envelope and wrote a note. I passed a note to a girl. Her mother and father worked with "troubled women" who were on drugs and helped them find Jesus and get clean.

They were nice to me. Whether they saw me as "pre-troubled" or just understood teenagers better, I don't know. I wanted to say good-bye. Why I thought this girl wouldn't tell her mother, I don't know. Probably I secretly wanted to be stopped. The girl gave it to her mother on Wednesday, the day after I planned to ride the bus to Bridgeport.

Tuesday, as I came home from school, outside my house was the familiar red station wagon of her mother. I was busted. What she told my mother, I don't know. That night I went to her house in her red wagon. I would eat and spend the night with the counselors, and the troubled women.

Before the rice and bean supper that night and before the prayer time as they agonized for my soul, we took a trip to her husband's office. After a short conversation with him, I was escorted into David Wilkerson's office. I was terrified.

Wilkerson was the man behind the book *The Cross and The Switchblade*. I knew of him. He often came to our church to preach. He had a reputation for being able to look through you and see your sinful soul. Friends had been called out by him because of their sins.

He looked at me with piercing eyes. His face was stern. He knew I had a plan to run away.

"How old are you, young lady?" I replied, *"I'm 14."*

With a disgusted shake of the head, he dismissed me. No offers of grace. No message that Jesus loved me. Not even a prayer with me, just disgust.

I saw him again many times as he preached from the pulpit of my church or churches in the neighborhood. I saw him when I was in a neighborhood youth choir at a neighboring Norwegian church. He looked at all the Norwegian youth in the choir and told us we needed to repent. Many did. Our parents prayed for revival. Most of those repenting were far more righteous than I.

That night after prayer and assurances that I wouldn't run away, they helped me with my geometry homework. I missed school the next day and was taken home. There was a promise of living with them in the future. I never made it to Bridgeport. I never lived with them either. But the plan to get the wayward child out of Brooklyn began to take shape.

It would seem logical to go to Long Island, Staten Island, New Jersey, or even upstate. That's where people went from Brooklyn. But not us. Waynesboro was the first choice.

Waynesboro is my mother's hometown. It's small. Nestled between the mountains, it is said that it got its name from the Revolutionary War hero, General Mad Anthony Wayne. Coming upon the valley he declared that it was a beautiful place for a town. It is.

Once a year, and occasionally twice, we would pack our suitcases and ride the subway to Penn Station. My dad helped with the suitcases as far as Penn Station. I never remember him going with us to Waynesboro. The train took us first to Trenton NJ, then to Philadelphia, and finally crossing the Susquehanna to the capitol city of Pennsylvania, Harrisburg.

While we were in Pennsylvania it was like my father didn't exist. Occasionally someone would ask about him. It seemed to me that many of my mother's family never quite understood why she married a foreigner.

We usually brought our lunch with us but in case one was hungry, a vendor would board the train in Philadelphia selling hard-boiled eggs and sandwiches. I would beg for a hard-boiled egg. They just tasted better when you bought them on the train. Frequent trips to the water fountain broke up the boredom of the trip. A cone-shaped cup filled with a swallow's worth of cold water tasted so good.

The conductor came through after each stop to check the tag at the edge of our seat. He punched holes and seemed to know immediately those that needed checking and those that didn't. There were interesting towns on the route – my favorite to hear was Paoli. The conductor would drag out the word PAAY-OOO-LI and sometimes add OLI, OLI, OLI. Still to come was Intercourse. Often my mother and I would talk about all the strange names of towns in Pennsylvania, like Intercourse, Fertility, Gravity, Prosperity, Rough and Ready, Noodle-Doozie, King of Prussia, Jim Thorpe, and Bird-in-Hand, to name a few.

Upon arrival in Harrisburg, we'd retrieve the suitcases that had been deposited over our heads by my father. Once off the train and in the station, we had our first glimpse of Armatha. Although there were times when I was much younger, we'd go first to my mother's sister Minnie, but most of my memories are seeing Armatha waiting for us in Harrisburg.

Armatha was not related. Yet among all the biological aunts and uncles I had, she still stands far above them all. Armatha was my mother's childhood friend. They had played together on Wayne Hill, went to church together, and had a bond that was deep and strong.

I was named after Armatha's only child, her daughter Joyce. She went by Joy most of her life. Shortly after I was born, Joy, about 17 years my senior, sent me a letter. I don't have it anymore, but she wrote to welcome her namesake into the world. Even though I barely knew her, I looked up to her. She was so beautiful and glamourous – so worldly and sophisticated.

Armatha loved to talk. Soon we'd be hearing about her family. She had a lot of siblings. They all seemed to have interesting nicknames like Bub and Skeeks, Neen and Sis, and several of them were called Potsy because her maiden name was Potts.

Armatha could cook! She made the most amazing, mashed potatoes. Everything tasted better at her table. My favorite after her mashed potatoes was a sandwich with Lebanon Bologna, mayo, fresh garden tomato, on a Martin's potato roll washed down by an ice-cold root beer in a glass bottle. Evenings were spent on her carport and capped off with a trip to the Dairy Twist for a dipped cone for me and a Mister Misty Float for my mother.

Unlike us, Armatha not only had a car but drove everywhere. She'd take us to track down my mother's siblings. She'd take us to Gettysburg to see the battlefield. She even took us to Hershey to see where the chocolate bars were made. At that time, you could tour the factory. Long before Willie Wonka, I fantasized walking through room after room of chocolate *conching* in large open vats. As we left at twilight, we'd watch the "kiss" shaped streetlights turn on. Trips to Waynesboro are some of my favorite memories of childhood. Until…

I was excited at the prospect of moving to Waynesboro. This seemed like a great answer to everyone's dilemma. I liked the area. I liked the schools. I liked the church. I even had friends there. My parents thought this might help their sinful daughter do better. However, I don't think my father was too keen on the idea.

I wrote a letter to one of my friends, Armatha's niece Lydia. In the letter, I told her that we might move and that while my mother thought I would just hang around with the church people, I was interested in having some fun too. BUSTED AGAIN. Armatha was told. My mother was told.

Although we did look at some apartments on our last trip to Waynesboro from Brooklyn, the plans for the move soon soured. On the way home, my mother told me that I had embarrassed her in front of all her friends. She said she was so embarrassed that she could never go to visit her family again. It was my fault. Why? Because of the letter I wrote to Lydia. Guilt. Failure. Shame. Seems I'd never be free or be enough.

That summer I went on a plane for the first time. Dressed in a cranberry-colored dress that I had made, we traveled by subway and NJ transit to Newark airport. There we boarded a flight to St. Louis Missouri. We were going to visit my oldest brother and his family for a week.

Seven people crammed in a 1967 Volkswagen beetle for the two-hour trip from Lambert Field to Columbia Missouri. Squeezed in the backseat with my mother and father, I peered out the window. My nephews were behind us in the storage well behind the back seat. Missouri looked like Pennsylvania because there were cows, but it was flatter and dryer.

My brother was completing a graduate degree and teaching at the University of Missouri. They lived in married student housing near campus. They took us on picnics and showed us Central Missouri. I ate my first pork tenderloin sandwich. It was delicious.

Often, when we stopped and all seven of us would emerge from the VW bug, people would stare at us. I remarked to my mother about the staring. I thought it was because there were so many of us. We looked like clown cars at the circus. She told me they likely stared because my brother's wife was Chinese.

I was shocked. It never occurred to me that anyone would stare because someone was a different nationality. That's how I saw it. Nationality. Not race. We were all just people from other places. Later, I would see my father marginalized or treated as an oddity in Missouri because of his accent.

Our trip ended with a visit to the St. Louis Zoo. I had my cranberry dress on again for travel. You dressed up to travel in those days. Standing at the gorilla cage, the giant was entertaining or perhaps punishing the crowd by taking his giant hand, cupping water, and sending it flying out over the crowd. It was hot and I suppose most didn't mind getting wet. Everyone was laughing.

However, the gorilla got me in my pretty dress. I cried while everyone laughed at me. I was going to have to travel on an airplane in a dress that had been drenched with gorilla water. I thought it was an omen of dreadful things to come. That was August.

A decision was made by September that we would pack our belongings and move to Columbia Missouri. I was 15. I was a Junior at John Jay High School in Brooklyn. We started school late that year due to a teachers' strike. After two weeks in eleventh grade, I was withdrawn from school, boarded a plane with my mother, and arrived again at Lambert Field.

I enrolled at Hickman High School. Due to differences in scheduling between NYC schools and Missouri schools, most of my classes were with Sophomores. School was quite different. No guards at the door, no captive lunch, and teachers who seemed to know their students and sometimes, even their families. I became a "Kewpie" – the school mascot. I learned the school song. And I turned sweet sixteen with a little cake at my brother's house before my dad joined us in Missouri.

My mother found a small house to rent. She bought a white 1969 VW beetle with the help of my brother. He helped her brush up on driving and get a Missouri driver's license. As soon as my dad arrived with the furniture, we settled into a little white stucco house on West Blvd South.

Change had come. Little did any of us know that more change was to come. Nor did we know how significant all those changes would be.

Wedding Bells

She is sixteen; she is a child.
She wears a satin dress.
She longs for love.
She holds her daddy's hand as she did as a child in Brooklyn.
She walks with him as so many strolls in a park lined with trees.
She feels the exhilaration of a push on a swing that takes her high,
          higher than the sky.
She feels the fear of climbing to the top of the monkey bars.
She hears music – it reminds her of the tune announcing the
          Mr. Softee truck – a treat awaits.
She hears music – it reminds her of Salem where she learned
          about Jesus.
A future awaits her.
Someone has chosen her; she must finally be worthy. She is
          finally wanted.
Her daddy hands her to the boy at the end of aisle.
Unknowingly, he has handed her to more rejection and abuse.
Scars upon scars,
wounds that can't heal,
voices of pain,
unworthy again.

FIVE

*P*erhaps it was the Viking in me, but I saw the move to Missouri as a great adventure. I missed Brooklyn. I missed all that was familiar, but I spent a lot of time exploring all my new surroundings. Life was different. Life seemed so much slower. Instead of walking through crowds of people, we got in the VW bug and rode. Initially, I rode the city bus to school, but I soon convinced my mother to "brave" driving me to school. Although I was 16, it would be years before I had my license.

I found that academically I was not as equipped as I should have been. Until High School, my education in New York City was superior. But I wasn't prepared for high school math. I struggled with geometry and PE. I couldn't pass the volleyball skill test. I did pass bowling and swimming. Finally, I passed PE. I passed geometry because of a good teacher and excelled in English and Spanish. History was never an issue. I liked Hickman but I was never connected like the students who had lived in Missouri all their lives.

We went to the local Assemblies of God church. That was logical. I wore my miniskirt. My mother got mad first at my skirts and second at a few of the old men in the church ogling me. The miniskirt might have been a minor problem in Brooklyn's churches but here in Missouri, at this church, it was a HUGE problem.

Under the watchful eye of the pastor and his wife, longer skirts, and longer sleeves were the standard. This was what holiness meant. Holiness was about how you dressed and whether you went to the movies or not. Make-up and TV were not part of the holiness standard either. Added to the list of the forbidden were women wearing pants (men's attire), alcohol, smoking, and swimming with members of the opposite sex, known as "mixed bathing." This was stricter than Brooklyn. I mixed bathed at Sunset Park and Coney Island all my life. I also wore dungarees, shorts, and pants.

Since the plan was to get me on the straight and narrow, my parents looked for a little less strict environment. The older I got the more autonomy I would have and therefore, they needed to keep me in church. My soul was at stake.

We traveled from church to church. We didn't go to the Catholic church but otherwise, we went to every other Christian denomination. Sunday meant a new church or a second trip to the one from the week before. We settled at a church for a month or two and then on to another.

One of the churches we settled on for a few months was the Columbia Church of God Holiness. And yes, it was also strict. They weren't Pentecostal. They were Wesleyan Holiness people. They were also very nice. They were not overbearing. People were friendly. I made some friends. We met a family that would ultimately become family. I don't remember why we left. But we did.

Just before our first Easter Sunday in Missouri, we went back to the First Assembly of God. That afternoon, the pastor's daughter, who I knew from school, and two other girls drove into our driveway. They wanted to take me to the Dairy Queen for ice cream. The invitation for a dipped cone drew me back to the church. I went back to church with them that night.

Maybe my skirt was a little longer on Easter Sunday, but I caught the attention of a boy. I was flattered. At 17 he came with a big Bible, sat on the very front row, and wore a suit. Every time the church doors were open, he was there. He asked me to go on a picnic on Easter Monday to "Pinnacle Bluffs."

I'm not, nor have I ever been "outdoorsy." I knew pants were out of the question. He was too holy to be attracted to a girl in pants. What to do? I wore a culotte dress. It was red polka dotted. It was pretty. I had made it. I also couldn't go to the bathroom without getting undressed. It was the only choice I had.

We brought some food and off we went through the woods. Besides having to go to the bathroom in the woods, the challenge of the day was walking across a log over a creek. Of course, I didn't make it. I was embarrassed. But the day did end with a kiss and a promise of more time together.

That day was about attention and insecurity. Perhaps I was not so undesirable that I could never find a husband. Imagine, one date and thinking about a husband. Perhaps it was echoes of the sense of a violation of my virtue that left me unworthy of marriage. My molester had told me things that while forgotten still echoed in my soul.

Allen was very charming. And he was a "super Christian." He believed in holiness. He was much beloved by the people of the church. He had grown up under their watchful eye. He had come with a neighbor to church as a child. His home life was not good. He clung to Jesus and the normalcy he found at church. I give Allen no excuses for the pain and abuse he ultimately inflicted. Nevertheless, nature and nurture shaped him into the person he became.

He didn't live with his parents. He was living in an apartment near the MU campus. He live on his own and went to the same high school as I did. Shortly after our trip in the woods the Monday after Easter, Allen lost his apartment and was relegated to the attic for lack of rent. The property owner benevolently let him put a bed on top of rafters and insulation. Moving because of lack of rent would happen to us repeatedly in years to come. We had a very brief courtship in the Spring of 1968. Talk of marriage escalated as a new place to live became necessary.

I became holy. I stopped wearing pants. I stopped hiding make-up. We still had a TV. My parents were happy to see me praying at the altar on Sunday night. They were thrilled I wanted to go to church on Wednesday night and Friday night youth service. If there was a "revival" I'd be there every night. Those revivals would go on for three weeks at a time with only Monday night off. My parents were ecstatic that I was doing hospital visitation on Saturday night and going to Missionettes regularly. The prodigal's return was working. The wayward daughter was secure.

As we did hospital visitation, one older woman would look at Allen and tell him he reminded her of Jesus. When we were alone, he did not act like Jesus though. He claimed a call to ministry. I dreamed of a future as a minister's wife. Validated and pure, I would finally be regarded as worthy.

Allen and I spent too much time alone. We were young and along with our passion for the Lord, we had passion for each other. He wanted to marry. I was 16, he 17. This seemed like a particularly good idea. My insecurities and self-image told me that if I didn't grab this one, no one else would ever want me. How lucky I was that finally, someone wanted me! The need to be wanted and the decisions I made because of it often controlled the direction of my life. Heaven knows, no one else would want me – or so my thinking went.

As predators usually do, he sensed my insecurities. Much later I found out he had dated other girls who were new in the church and seemed insecure. He was on the prowl, on the hunt. He wanted to marry. Why? I'm not sure. Maybe a place to live. We thought we were old enough to know what we wanted to do. I succumbed to my insecurities thinking I had better jump at the chance to get married while I could.

Our first date was April 17, 1968. By May 1968, we had plans to marry. I wanted to be a June bride. My parents asked me to wait until July. When

I got married their Social Security income would be cut in half. We agreed.

We both had to have a parent sign permission for us to legally marry. Both mothers went independently to the county courthouse giving their consent to our marriage. Later, my mother told me she cried on the way home. She said she had some fleeting thoughts about destroying my life.

Why didn't she listen to those thoughts? My mother thought I was pregnant. I wasn't. If I were pregnant, the sin would be covered by marriage. I'm sure the refrain of "*what will people think*" drowned out the doubts and concern for my future. The week before I got married, I had my period. PROOF. Immediately, my mother took me to a doctor for birth control.

My father didn't say much. I think he may have been heartbroken. He wanted me to go to college. But more than that, he wanted me to be right with Jesus and heading for heaven. He would console himself with comments about me and my dolls. He was thinking of those long walks in Brooklyn pushing the grey doll pram and giving attention to my "baby." He concluded that I was destined to be a wife and mother. Allen was a nice Christian boy. I was now right with Jesus and a good husband would help keep the unwanted sinful daughter in the fold.

My mother started sewing my wedding gown. It was a white satin A-line dress in a similar pattern to the cranberry one the Gorilla soaked the summer before. It had white satin bows on the shoulder. The long sleeves ended in a point past my wrist, and a very long train. It was modest and extremely hot for a July wedding.

Tuesday, July 2, 1968, at 7:00 p.m. I walked the aisle with my arm in my dad's and was handed over to become Mrs. Allen Lynch. We said I do. We knelt together pledging our lives to God's service, His glory, and each other. We had a cake and punch reception and headed to the "Lake of the Ozarks" in a decorated 1951 Chevy with three on the column. Our first stop was a motel in Jefferson City. Friends followed us to the door of the motel.

The people of the church were loving. Even if they did think I was pregnant or weren't sure about me, they did bless us in so many ways. The pastor's wife worked hard to make sure I had a nice wedding. This was a gift she had. Many girls from the church will testify to her generosity. She also hosted a "personal shower." For a very conservative church, there was an irony about having holiness women sitting in the parsonage admiring the new bras, underwear, and sexy nightwear I was given at the shower.

Our cake and punch reception was held in the Fellowship Hall of the church. The women of the church rallied to provide a nice reception including the little nuts and mints that always appeared at weddings. Two long tables were covered with gifts to help us as we launched into our new life.

I am sure one of the wedding gifts I got at the reception was an electric skillet. It was the microwave of its day. You can cook almost anything in it. I used it to make all manner of burgers, sauces, pancakes and more. Armed with my Betty Crocker cookbook, also a wedding gift, I practiced with diligence to be a good wife. I rarely offered up burnt offerings to my new husband. I also entertained.

One time I invited the visiting evangelists to our home. It was expected that people of the church invite them to a home cooked evening meal before the service. I prepared lasagna and salad topped with a homemade cake and coffee. The wife marveled at my willingness to host them in our tiny trailer home. She was shocked that I knew how to make a good cup of percolated coffee at 16.

The other gift I remember so clearly was the gift that I thought was the best wedding gift I had received. It was a bucket. Yes, a bucket – it was filled with brushes, sponges, dish rags and all manner of kitchen gadgets, peelers, a paring knife, and more. It was a gift from Sister Sanders, the mother of my husband's best friend. She said I'd need those things. And indeed, it contained the things I needed the most.

I was set. I was playing house with greater expertise than the average 16-year-old would have. I looked forward to the life of a preacher's wife. Allen was already working on credentials with the Assemblies of God. He got them. We thought about being evangelists until we were experienced enough to pastor.

In preparation for our upcoming wedding, we rented a small house and cleaned it spotless. We never lived in it. Allen wanted to buy a home. He found a trailer for sale. It was just a small camper. The outside was red and white and measured 8-foot by 28-foot. In that tiny space it had a bathroom, bedroom, kitchen and living room. It even had full size appliances.

We parked our trailer in a trailer court next to Donnie and Lannie Roper, a college couple we knew from church. Somehow, even though just a few years older, they seemed so much wiser. They were good neighbors. They lived so close they would hear me when I cried at night.

I waited for my next monthly cycle so I could start taking birth control pills. It never came. I was pregnant.

SIX

*I*t's hard to explain emotional abuse. I suppose I was an easy target. It usually works that way. Someone insecure finds an even more insecure person to control and manipulate. He seemed so secure to me. He seemed to know what he wanted. He had a certain charm about him with his baby face. In church, people liked him.

I was a child. I had no business being married. I thought I was in love. Maybe I was? I know without any doubt that ultimately, I loved him. Only those we love deeply can inflict the levels of pain I endured from him. Love is like that, the more you love, the more you are vulnerable to great pain.

I was far from the streets of Brooklyn living in a small camper trying to play house with a boy who belittled and derided me constantly. I thought this would be different. I would be good enough. He had chosen me.

He had a job and made money. He bought the best tools and best clothes. I wore things people gave me. My clothes came from older women in the church. A year before I was sporting cute miniskirts like a normal teenager. Now I was dressed in floral shirtwaist dresses that were cast offs from women old enough to be my grandmother.

In addition to the ministry, he wanted to be a carpenter. He hung dry wall and did framing to bring in some money. Friday being payday, he was always late. It wasn't a bar that lured him. He was too holy for that. It was new clothes from the finest men's shop in Columbia or new tools at the hardware store. He always had to have the best. Food for our table was optional. After a shower, we'd scurry to young people's meeting at the church. Still children, we still belonged to the youth group.

I don't remember the order of the first two physical abuse episodes. All abuse seems to start subtly. Like Mr. Thompsen grooming me with candy, an abuser never shows their true colors quickly. First, they pick you. How thrilled you are to be picked; first by Mr. Thompsen and his candy treats. Now I had been picked by Allen and his offers of love and respectability.

They pick you because you are insecure and starved for love and attention. They make you feel as if they are your savior. They are the ones who can make your life better. You'll do anything to please them; control is amazingly easy.

In your desire to please and feel significance, you believe that you really are inadequate. The problem is you. If only you could do things better, you would be loved and appreciated. If you could just perform well, your abuser will love you more.

Add God to this mix and you have a perfect recipe for abuse. I wanted more than anything to please God. I also wanted to atone for all the sins of my youth. I didn't really have that many, but I felt guilty. Works-based righteousness will do that to you. My husband, now the head of the house and the one to whom I was to submit, told me I was lacking, severely lacking.

The first slap across the face left me stunned. I cried for hours. Our neighbors heard me. They were alarmed. It was summer and the windows were open. They heard the slap as our living room was but a few feet from their bedroom. Nevertheless, they were afraid to come to my aid. Eventually I went next door and knocked on their door. They were awake and dressed. Later the wife shared they were staying awake in case I needed something, or he hit me again.

Eventually I apologized to him for what I had done wrong that resulted in the slap. Begging for forgiveness, I was granted another chance to be a good wife. At night, in bed, he would punch my swelling pregnant breasts. He said it reminded him of bread rising from yeast and he thought it was fun to punch it down.

No one knew. I told no one. I was the person who needed to change. I was the one who needed to atone for my sins. If only I were a better wife. It was my fault.

My mother-in-law Esther thought I should go to work. She said she had always worked. She had no sympathy for our lack of food in the house. It didn't matter to her that we went without. She felt I should work. I tried. I had several jobs during those first few months as Mrs. Allen Lynch.

In Brooklyn, my mother had worked as a caregiver for a wealthy family. The man was much older than his wife. They lived in a Penthouse overlooking Prospect Park. She would help him with bathing and basic care. My mother got along well with the wife.

The first year in Missouri she got a job at the local Catholic school as a helper in the kitchen. She liked the job. The environment was stressful. She quit after one month. Because of her example, I didn't think I should have to work. I was pregnant. I was a homemaker now.

Married women were to be like the role models of Donna Reed, June Cleaver, or the "bewitched" Samantha Stephens. I wasn't lazy. I told someone recently that I still hear the tape of my mother-in-law. She is telling me again how lazy I am. So powerful were those words that at times, I still believe her.

Getting a job at 16 was not easy. I had no clerical skills. I didn't know how to type. I knew neither Gregg nor Pitt stenography. Most of the summer jobs were given to people who knew people, children of a friend. I eventually landed a job at a drug store on Broadway, the core business street in bustling downtown Columbia.

I bought a hairnet to wear. I must have worn some sort of uniform, although I don't remember it. I was going to work at the lunch counter. I was supposed to take orders and make drinks. This included mastering the skill of making a *Lime Rickey* (a limeade). I would cut the limes and press out the juice. Add some sugar syrup and add the seltzer. The pay was about 75 cents an hour. I wasn't allowed to have tips.

I remember it only so vaguely now. I didn't work there for long. I do remember Mr. Peters came in several times while I worked there. He was the business teacher at Hickman and the father of friends from church. His smile was the only memorable thing about this experience. There can be great power in a simple smile. I don't remember why I quit. Likely it was transportation. I didn't know how to drive. We didn't live on a bus line. Or it could have been vanity, they did make me wear a hairnet.

Another time that summer, I got a job at a magazine distribution warehouse. I think I lasted two days. Lifting heavy stacks of magazines was required. Lifting heavy objects was something I felt would jeopardize my pregnancy. I quit. My husband told me about someone he knew that was picking watermelons in a field before they went into labor. She returned to the field shortly after delivery. I heard similar stories from his mother. She continue to call me lazy and tell me I should work.

My mother would buy us groceries. I had halved their income and yet somehow, she always found a way to help put food on my table. We had a dog as well. My mother was not keen on that dog, but she bought it food regularly. Then she would ask what is wrong with Allen? Isn't he working? I would say yes and repeat his comments about how you had to spend money to make it. I would tell her that he had bought a new saw, or a new tool belt, or some other top-of-the-line tool for his trade. I told her I asked him why he had to have the most expensive and he would say "I just have to." She would shake her head in disgust.

Before there were food stamps, there were commodity foods. I signed up for them. Our pantry now had large cans labeled government surplus food. The butter in the can was wonderful. I became proficient in creating ways to use the powdered eggs and canned chicken, pork, and beef. I never liked beans so I would often trade them with someone else for another can of peanut butter.

I was now part of the system. All the things that people thought of me were coming true. I was a poor pregnant teenager who was now getting free food and begging for food from her mother. I was always the one who had to go ask for help. He had too much pride.

No matter where I turned, everyone was unhappy with me. The monster of insecurity was claiming every aspect of my soul. The situation was so ripe for more abuse. It is only through reflection, with the perfection of hindsight, that I see that every day I was subject to increasing emotional and verbal abuse. Physical violence would appear sporadically.

Sometimes our talk in that little trailer would turn to the child I was carrying. We talked of names. I wanted a boy. I wanted to give my husband a son. Somehow, it seemed the better of the two choices, a son, or a daughter.

I don't remember Allen saying much about a girl's name. I chose Hannah Marie. His mother hated the name and would just say – Hard Hearted Hannah, that's a terrible name. Allen did have a choice for a boy's name, Nature. I hated the idea. I wanted Bible names. Using the scripture as my weapon, I won. We chose Nathaniel Karl. Karl is a name that runs through my family on my father's side.

There was a problem with the name Nathaniel. My father, with his still strong Norwegian accent couldn't say Nathaniel. His tongue twisted over the name. I decided we couldn't name our child a name his grandfather couldn't say. We chose Nicholas. That, he could say. Oh, the dreams I had for my child as I would lay in that little trailer. I instinctually knew it was a boy. I don't remember dreaming of anything but a son.

My prenatal care came from the University hospital. People without insurance could receive prenatal care there. I had no idea about insurance. I just knew there was a clinic there. Medical students and residents examined and poked me at Clinic 7.

I was required to have a shot of penicillin each month. They told me it was because of a heart murmur they heard. Having had Rheumatic Fever as a child they were unsure of what this murmur meant. They felt antibiotics were necessary.

With my bare butt exposed, I asked a scowling nurse why I had to have an injection each month. Her reply was that I couldn't be trusted to take a pill. Like a macabre retribution for my teenage pregnancy, she thrust the needle in my hip. I will never forget that nurse. Dressed in starched white with a strange pill-box nurses cap, she seemed evil.

I suppose the murmur was serious. After delivery I had to visit the cardiac clinic number 4. Fortunately, the murmur disappeared once my child was born. I never had to have injections or even oral antibiotics with subsequent pregnancies.

Loser, a term I've heard a lot in my life. Even today, like "you're lazy" it resonates in me. I wonder when I will no longer be a lazy loser. The adage about sticks and stones and names never hurting is not true. Words stick. Words hurt. Sometimes they echo through the soul even when the mind knows they are untrue.

I went back to Hickman to complete my senior year. I remember the look on the teacher's face when I gave her the note excusing me from PE. She had been nice to me when I first came to Columbia. She seemed disappointed and surprised. What had been her opinion of me before? I don't know. I don't even know what her look meant. I just know she had a reaction unlike most of the teachers. It was less distain and more a look of disappointment.

I quit school. This was the first of three times I was a drop-out. I turned my attention again to being a good wife. I was preparing to be a mother.

April 1, April Fool's Day, was the due date. At seven months pregnant, on February 8th, I woke up spotting. Allen had gone to do some work for someone out in the country. I didn't know where they lived, and I didn't know if they had a phone. I went to the neighbor and used the phone to call my mother. She came. We went to the ER at the University of Missouri Medical Center.

They took me to the Maternity floor. I was told to undress. I wasn't given a gown; I was told just take off your panties. I had a skirt on. A very austere tall female resident walked in. From the instant she walked in, I felt scorn. She directed me to the exam table and placed my feet in the stirrups.

She asked a few questions while examining me. She said, *"You are fine. It's not a big deal."* Then she walked out the door. I did the logical thing and put my panties back on and waited. She didn't say I could leave. My mother wasn't in the room to ask.

The door opened. Two middle aged men in white coats came into the room. The first thing they did was scold me for getting dressed. I stepped behind a curtain to remove my underwear again. I climbed back onto the table.

I was fighting tears. I was scared. No one talked nicely to me. Donned with their gloves, they put their hands inside me. They treated me very rough. Being so young, with no prior experiences, I felt molested. There was no concern for the discomfort. Then I heard one of them say, *"I feel a foot."*

After more discussion and prodding, they decided to send me to X-Ray to get a better look at the baby. The resident was tasked with accompanying me. She pushed me down the hall and into the elevator. I was laying on a hard stretcher. I cried.

After the X-Ray I was admitted to the Labor Room. It was determined that a foot had descended. They would wait to see if I started active labor. Allen came and we walked down the hallway. We could see the X-Ray hanging in an adjacent room. You could clearly see that foot dangling, ready to come out into the world.

I attempted to sleep in the green Labor Room. Occasionally a nurse would come in to check on me. I woke up frequently. I would pray for my baby. Morning came. I felt some odd sensations. I didn't know I was in labor because I had no idea what that would be like. I was:

> Alone
> > Scared
> > > Waiting
> > > > Wondering
> > > > > Would my child be born alive?
> > > > > Would it be painful?

Seventeen and about to give birth attended by people who viewed me as trash.

A very young medical student came in to ask all the questions I had already answered multiple times. I remember him. He was different. He was the first person who treated me with some respect. He was kind. And he stayed with me most of the day. Those sensations I was having were contractions.

On Sunday evening, February ninth, I was wheeled into delivery. The room was overwhelming and frightening. It was filled with people. The male doctors who had examined me the day before were at my feet. My feet were high in the stirrups. The door opened. Twenty surgically masked men walked in the room. I was told they were there to observe since I was having an unusual birth.

Nicholas arrived feet first. He was whisked away to be examined. My mother made phone calls that created a buzz of comments such as:

I knew she must have been pregnant when she got married.

I always knew the girl was trash.

I knew what they were saying and thinking.

I couldn't hold him. I couldn't touch him. I barely saw him as they whisked him off to the NICU.

As I looked at him through several layers of glass, I saw he had no fingernails or toenails. He had no eyelashes or brows. He had a tube down his throat for nourishment, as he did not know how to suck yet. It was a month before I held him and even then, the nurses found ways to scorn and deride me.

Nicholas was over three weeks old when I was finally able to hold him for the first time. I had no way to go to the hospital except when my mother took me. When I did get there, I would only look longingly at him through several layers of glass. Years later, with yet another child in an incubator, they let me scrub, and reach my gloved hand into the holes to touch her. This time, no courtesy like that was permitted.

The day came when he was no longer in the NICU. His tubes were removed. He could suck. He still had no eyebrows, but fingernails were forming. At church people were reconsidering whether my story of his premature birth was true. He finally weighed five pounds.

An older nurse working in the regular nursery was sitting in a rocking chair, holding him, and giving him a bottle. I had thought about breast-feeding. I knew no one that breastfed. It just seemed natural to me. I didn't know then how much better it is for the new infant. I just thought I'd like to try to do it. No one told me I could pump milk. No one gave me any information. It was assumed he'd be fed with a bottle.

As I went in, the nurse frowned. She had that look. By now, I knew it well. I was young. Too young to be married and mother. Obviously, I had to get married. I was just another loser and immoral girl trying to atone for her sins by getting married. She asked, "*Do you want to feed your baby?*" Did I? **Of course, I did.**

Carefully and cautiously with emotions too strong to put into words, I took him in my arms for the first time. The nurse, still scowling, showed me how to hold him. She showed me how to hold the bottle. I knew how to do all those things as I had practiced for years with my dolls and later with real babies in the church nursery. I knew I had to burp him at some time. I put him on my shoulder, patting his back. No burp. I tried again. Still no burp.

I was told by one of them to put the baby on my lap and rub his head. They told me that rubbing the top of his head would make him burp. Even though I thought it strange, I did it. He burped. I suppose the nurses had a good laugh at my expense when I left. I saw the snickering looks being exchanged by the two nurses in the room. Despite being the butt of their jokes, I was ecstatic.

My mother came looking for me. She didn't see me with nose pressed to the glass. Finally, she saw me sitting in a rocking chair beaming. Finally, there was a baby in my arms.

It took another week before he was stable enough to go home. I had no crib or bassinette for him. He slept first in a dresser drawer and then a laundry basket. I had some clothes and diapers. Diapers were cloth. From then on, the faint smell of urine would pervade the air in that trailer. Diapers would be swished in a toilet to remove the solid waste. Laundry would pile high as it waited for a spin at the local Laundromat. Transportation always came from my mother in the beloved 1969 white Volkswagen.

We moved. I don't remember why we moved or what ever happened to that camper. We may have planned to make payments on it and didn't. We may have gotten behind in our lot rent and abandoned it. I really don't know.

Packing our meager belongings into our 1951 Chevy *tanklike* vehicle, we moved to another trailer. This one was bigger than the last but old. It was in town. Allen didn't like living in town. We were near the interstate and could hear the trucks day and night. Allen was a country boy. Before the song "Thank God I'm a country boy," he was true to its meaning. I, born and raised in Brooklyn NY, we couldn't have been more mismatched. I tried to be country. I tried to learn his ways. I chose the wedding song *Wither Thou Goest* as one of our songs. I meant it. I was determined to be a wonderful wife. Our new address was 52 Rainbow Village. Rainbows, the sign of promise, must mean life was going to get better. I thought we had moved up in status.

As a child, I had learned that the better I could perform, the more love I would get. Now even my attempts at performance did not reciprocate with love. I still couldn't do anything right. No matter how much I cooked, cleaned, washed, it was never enough. When his underwear wasn't folded to his standards, he would get very angry. I never thought you had to fold underwear!

Abuse would continue despite living in *Rainbow* Village. He had a new target. The laundromat in the trailer court was convenient. I went to check on some clothes and hang them on the line outside the laundromat. Returning to the trailer, the sound of a baby crying in terror could be heard as I walked up to the trailer door. I rushed in. Nicholas' left cheek was bright red with the outline of a handprint. I picked him up and asked, *"did you hit him?"* He said, *"he wouldn't shut up."*

I should have left. That's easy to say now. I only remember saying *"he's a baby, you don't hit a baby."* He said something about teaching him to obey.

I was no longer the only target of physical abuse. I told my mother. She was appalled but never told me to leave. She said just don't leave the house without the baby. She didn't know what to do either.

At church, people remarked with great wonder that he was so small. I suppose I don't really know what those remarks meant. To me, I heard - maybe she wasn't pregnant when she got married after all. On Easter Sunday, April 6, 1969, we presented him in a white suit with blue embroidery on the shirt saying, **"I'M A BOY"** to be dedicated to the Lord. My first date with Allen was Easter Monday April 17, 1968 – in one short year, I was married, and a mother.

At Sunday night services, as we would go to the altars to pray and solidify the message in our hearts, I would place a receiving blanket on the mourner's bench. I would lay Nicholas on top of it, as I knelt in prayer and prayed for him. I prayed that he would be a great man of God someday. I prayed that I would be a good mother.

About that time, someone broke all the side windows of our 1951 Chevy. Allen said it was an angry customer at the burger place where he worked. It was still cold in Columbia as we would drive where we needed to go with open windows on all sides. I would wrap Nicholas in many blankets and shiver as we went to church, to see his mother, and anywhere else we needed to go. Car seats weren't required so I clutched him as close as I could.

I was still in love. Or so I thought. I have a child now. I had to do better. I had to be a good wife. If only I could do better, things would be wonderful.

At times, Allen would send me to the other room to repent for things he felt I had done. I would dutifully go to the other room, bend my knee, asking God to forgive me. My sins and disobedience were the thing preventing our future as a happy Christian couple, preaching the gospel.

SEVEN

I don't know how many places we lived after Rainbow Village. We were always moving because of unpaid rent or just because he thought he'd found a better deal. One of the places we moved to be his mother's trailer. Fortunately, we didn't live there very long either.

My mother-in-law Esther was a large woman. She was not much taller than I was, but I felt she towered over me. She was married to a man named Geoffrey and they lived in a shack in "Lindbergh." The shack was covered with asphalt siding. The trailer we lived in was next to her shack. She had bought it as an investment.

Lindbergh was an unincorporated community on what had been the main road to get to St. Louis. After the interstate was finished, it saw only local traffic. Lindbergh had a one store that sold everything in a very tight space. Items of necessity were stacked to the ceiling. Several large white deep freezers lined the wall. They held meat of unknown origin and ice cream. An old soda machine kept the soft drinks cold. Candy bars and bags of chips provided quick snacks. Behind the cashier were rows of cigarettes, chewing tobacco, and snuff. Fishing bait, sundries, and over-the-counter medications lined the other shelves. It was a mini-Wal-Mart.

There were about ten homes in Lindbergh. One house was very nice, and a wonderful woman named Vesta lived in it. She was the "Grande Dame" of Lindbergh. Vesta was tall and carried herself with confidence. Every Sunday she gathered the children of the neighborhood in her car to take them to church. She had beautiful snow-white hair. Every Christmas she would don a white robe and wings to play the angel at the church Christmas pageant.

The worst house in Lindbergh belonged to my mother-in-law. I wasn't prepared for my first visit to her house. There were two doors that gave access to the house from the driveway. One door led to the screened-in porch and then to the kitchen. The other accessed the living room. I always preferred that door.

The living room had the usual recliner and floral sofa. Multiple crocheted afghans draped over the furniture. The large gas heater provided the heat for the house. In the poorly lit room, it gave a warm glow. It was the centerpiece of the living room. It kept the living room too hot and provided little heat to other parts of the shack. A large wooden console television completed the living room. I don't ever remember being in the living room when the television wasn't on. I do remember watching some of the multiple cats supplement the entertainment of the night as they attempted to torment and catch a mouse in front of the glowing heater.

As you entered the house through the screened-in porch, you were greeted by the mice sculptured cakes that were always on top of the deep freeze. Esther would bring home discount cakes from the grocery store. Sometimes they were simple pound cakes, other times they were decorated birthday cakes that didn't sell. The mice always got them first. The ever-present mice had dug out tunnels in the cakes. Often you could see them still at work eating their way through the cake or bread or anything on top of the white chest freezer. Everything was sprinkled with roaches in every stage of development.

The only refrigerator was also on this porch. The refrigerator door latch was broken. A padlock *hasp* kept the door closed. Going through the porch you arrived in the kitchen. A large wooden table occupied most of the space. The table was next to the washing machine connected to the sink. The hose for the wastewater was placed through a window. The hose delivered the water to the front yard.

The bathroom attached to the kitchen had no light fixtures. It did had a window. During the daytime you could see where the roaches and the mice were. At night, it was a different story. The bathtub was usually black unless someone cleaned it for a bath. I never knew what made it so black. I did everything I could to avoid going into that bathroom at night.

The bathroom was a relatively new addition. The outhouse was still in the back of the house. Esther had the bathroom installed in the house. For months after it was installed, Geoffrey refused to use it preferring the familiarity of the outhouse. Likewise, Geoffrey took his laundry to the laundromat because he objected to the washing machine.

Esther had decided to raise rabbits for research labs. She had read somewhere this was a get-rich-quick scheme. The University Medical Center in Columbia was always doing research. They would certainly buy rabbits from her. It was perfect. She'd be rich.

The rabbit cages were all over her house; their droppings fell to the carpet. They made the house smell. She could never understand why I would clutch my infant son Nicholas so tightly when we would be in their house. She would tell me to make a pallet (folded blanket) and put him on the floor. I couldn't. I wouldn't.

One day we were summoned for Sunday dinner with my mother-in-law and Geoffrey. The propane gas stove was filled with dishes cooking under the watchful eye of Esther. She was a cook by trade.

As we sat down to eat, there was fried meat on the table. I had long since mastered the skill of cutting a whole chicken and frying it for supper. This was not a chicken. There were green beans with potatoes flavored with salt pork. Biscuits, gravy and other standard fare graced the table.

We crowded around the feast she had prepared. What was I going to do? I knew I had to eat. The safest thing on the table was the potatoes and green beans. While overcooked and unappealing, they were the best option. I knew I had to eat the meat. I knew if I didn't, I would be disrespectful to Esther. In addition to the harangue, I would get from her, Allen would continue it when we went back to our trailer next door. There was no escape.

Like the cats that tormented the mice in her living room, she started. She shoved the meat in front of my face. I took a piece. She said take another. I did. She smiled. Nicholas was on my lap. Almost like a security blanket or a defense shield, I clutched him tightly. I was thankful he was too young to be given meat. I broke a small bite of potato and put it in his mouth.

I pushed things around on my plate for a while. I was examining the bone structure. Like a culinary trivia game, I studied to determine its origin. I had no idea.

She must have known I was uncomfortable. After all, I was that city-girl, the uppity one. Finally, I tasted it. It wasn't too bad. I just wasn't sure what I was eating. That bothered me a lot. Once she knew I had tasted her creation, she asked me how I liked it. I lied and said it was very good. Then she asked me, *"Do you know what it is?"* I said *"no, I don't."*

She had me. She was ready for the kill. She knew I was afraid of her. She had planned this.

"It's a squirrel. Geoffrey went hunting and killed him a squirrel. It's good, isn't it?" Fighting the surge of nausea, I smiled and said *"yes."* She continued, *"I bet you ain't never had squirrel before?"* I fought to keep the food coming up in my throat from landing on the plate in front of me. I said, *"No."*

She started to laugh. Her laugh reminded me of the mechanical woman outside a fun house on the Coney Island boardwalk. It was the sound of an evil and maniacal laugh that fit her bipolar personality. I feared for what was next. Her scorn was always harsh, but this laugh signaled something worse.

"Hell, that ain't no squirrel." It seemed everyone was in on the joke. Her evil laugh reached a new pitch and as if on cue, everyone else at the table was laughing.

"You thought you were eating squirrel!!" More laughter erupted. I moved my chair away from the table slightly. I wondered if there was a way to escape. She continued, *"That's one of them there rabbits I raise. It died."*

Now maybe rabbit wasn't as bad as thinking it was a squirrel. I knew people ate squirrels occasionally, but I also knew that more people ate rabbit. I thought, don't the French eat rabbit? It seemed a better option but what did it die from? I am sure no one knew and that really bothered me. Should I go to the ER and tell them I ate fried rabbit and the rabbit likely died from living in filth?

While I attempted to ponder what to do next, I heard her say, *"So, I cooked it. I have a few others frozen in the freezer. I'll give you one to take home."*

The frozen rabbit sat in the back of my freezer for a long time. Too afraid to throw it away but never planning to eat it, it just sat there. Sometimes I wondered if it really was a rabbit. It looked like it could have been a cat. One never knew with these folks.

I managed to find a way to never eat there again. Nevertheless, we continued to visit. She was my mother-in-law. Nicholas was her grandchild. They were now my family.

EIGHT

*A*llen had finished high school just before we married. He was a year older and a year ahead of me. As my class, Hickman 1969, donned their caps and gowns, I was preparing for yet another move. Having passed the test for his exhorter's credentials with the Assemblies of God, we packed our belongings for our first major move to Neosho Missouri, the flower box city 242 miles away. Neosho was to be the home of the new Ozark Bible Institute (OBI).

Neosho, only 76 miles from the international headquarters of the Assemblies of God, was at odds with its denomination. Worldliness had crept into the Assemblies in the form of lipstick, eye shadow, television, short hair, short sleeves, mixed bathing, and all manner of sinful behavior. Their quarrel was not doctrine. Its quarrel were standards. They would teach only the Bible proclaiming *Without Holiness No Man Shall See the Lord.* Allen was to be in the first class at OBI.

We found an apartment on the second floor of a house on College Street. The small three-room apartment shared a bathroom with a room lent out to an older man from time to time. The plan was that I would work and help support Allen through school. The apartment was convenient. I could walk to downtown or to church. A Laundromat was on the corner. Rows of clotheslines for drying your clothes were available behind the building. I saved the money on the dryer and hung out the clothes. All our underwear and the baby's diapers were on display as people entered town.

Our landlady, a pleasant but opinionate woman did childcare in her home. They were worldly folk with a television. They didn't like the holiness people. They didn't understand why being Baptist was not enough for heaven. Nevertheless, our landlady had more compassion for me than most people.

I was a 17-year-old high school dropout with a child. Once settled, I began my job search. I would walk the square in Neosho day in and day out. There were many stores on the square, and I persisted in visiting each store many times.

If I had money, my landlady would watch Nicholas while I begged for a job. Other times, I carried him with me as I walked downtown to beg.

Finally, the owner of a drugstore got sick of seeing me. He told me he'd hire me on a trial basis for 25 cents an hour. If I worked out, he'd give me the normal pay of 50 cents an hour. It was our landlady who convinced me that I couldn't afford to work for that. It wouldn't cover the babysitting.

We couldn't afford formula for Nicholas. He was too young for regular milk. I followed a recipe I found for homemade formula. Using evaporated milk, adding corn syrup and water, I made "formula." Evaporated milk was cheap. Even so, I would have to collect soda bottles for refunds and pennies to have enough to buy just a few cans of milk to feed our son. Allen found a job working nights at the Buddy L plant. He made barbeque grills. He would go to school during the day and work at night.

I decided to try high school again. I enrolled in Neosho High School. As a married woman, I wore only holiness standard clothing. Only a single woman could wear her hair down. I would secure my hair tightly in a bun or a French roll. My face scrubbed, I attempted to blend in with the class of 1970. Again, I took typing. The typewriters were all manual uprights. There were no letters on the keys to assure we learned to touch type on the QWERTY keyboard. Pounding the keys, I thought someday maybe I could get a decent job as a secretary.

The evening of July 16, 1969, as we came home from the Wednesday evening church service, our landlady called to us. She asked us to come in. She said we shouldn't miss history being made. Allen, ever holy, forbid television watching. We had just left church.

This Baptist temptress was luring us to forbidden territory. Live coverage of Neal Armstrong's stepping off the lunar module, the Eagle, was the bait. Ever sinful and prone to temptation, I begged to stay. We did. Nicholas was placed on a pallet on her clean floor. I sat on the couch. Allen clutched the doorknob still struggling in his soul with this sinful behavior. We watched the first moonwalk.

I had watched on the school television rolled into our classroom by the AV team, all the precursors to this day. In fuzzy black and white I saw Shepherd blast off into space. I had watched with wide eyes as John Glenn splashed down after orbiting the earth. I was so glad I didn't miss the winning lap of the race to the moon.

Allen decided he didn't need Bible School after all. Back to Columbia we went. This time to another upstairs apartment west of Columbia over less hospitable landlords. My parents had moved to subsidized senior housing at Garth Towers. I was a frequent, too frequent guest in their home. We were thrown out of our apartment for lack of rent. We stayed with my parents. They were on the verge of being asked to leave because of our presence. My parents decided to rent a house that we could share. Our next stop was 909 Wilkes Blvd.

I got pregnant again. It was 1970. The Viet Nam war was raging. Uncle Sam promised money, insurance, and security in return for service. Allen decided it was time to do his duty for God and country. Despite his deferment, he enlisted.

Underneath I was terrified. I was terrified I'd be a widow. Yet, there was another, even darker feeling lurking deep below. The abuse had already taken its toll. I knew divorce was out of the question. Christians were forbidden to divorce. I was sure divorce would solidify forever my place in Hell. In horror at times, I would think that maybe he would go to Viet Nam and be killed. I'd be free. I'd be a widow, but I'd be free.

As if she knew, my mother-in-law would at times scream at me her own fears of Viet Nam. She would say he's going to get killed and it's all your fault. I would cry. I would beg God to forgive me for these horrible thoughts.

He went to Basic. As Johnny Carson would come on the television each night, I would write long letters on blue stationery sprayed with cheap perfume telling him the activities of the day, pledging my fidelity and love.

Death was around the corner - my great ally and support had gotten sick. He soon would be gone.

NINE

*A*llen enlisted and went to Fort Leonard Wood for Basic. I took the Greyhound bus with Nicholas to visit. I stayed in the guesthouse for the weekend. Allen wasn't supposed to have visitors during Basic Training, but I took Greyhound anyway. We had no car, and I didn't have a driver's license so I couldn't borrow my mother's VW.

The room we were in had bunk beds and was adequate. I saw Allen for a few hours but overall, the trip was a bus ride and sleeping on a bunk. The highlight was my sweet little boy. I remember sitting on the bottom bunk teaching Nicholas to point to his eyes, nose, and mouth on command. I thought he must be the smartest child that ever lived!

Another baby was already growing in my belly. Soon there would be two. A woman at church who was also a military dependent was teaching me the ins and outs of military life. She decided we should go shopping on post. We went to the commissary to buy groceries. I had never shopped at a military commissary or a PX, so this was good training. On the way home, we had a harrowing trip in a blizzard. We rode behind a snowplow following its tracks as snow covered the freezing roadway.

Finally, I went to his graduation from Basic. I was very proud of him. He looked great in his uniform, and I thought maybe things would turn around. He came home for a short leave. My stomach continued to grow. He moved on to AIT, Advanced Infantry Training, at Fort Polk Louisiana. The welcome sign at Fort Polk declared it was the training ground for Viet Nam. Fear gripped my soul again.

I bought a Greyhound bus ticket again. If he was going to end up in Viet Nam, I had to spend as much time as possible with him. I was determined to be a good and supportive wife. I was Louisiana bound.

I had no idea that this was frowned upon and probably not appreciated by the Army. I spent the weekend mostly alone in a guesthouse. On Sunday, we rode an old school bus to an Assemblies of God church in Leesville. The young pastor gave us the use of his car for the day. We drove around the swampy environs of Leesville enjoying our day of freedom. We returned the car to him after the Sunday night service. The next day I boarded a Trailways bus for the return trip. Both Nicholas and

I took Dramamine to sleep. It probably wasn't a good idea. I didn't know any better.

Back in Columbia, my father was sick. Something wasn't right. He went to the ER. At 19, I thought my father old at 71. It was his gall bladder. In 1971, gall bladder surgery was routine. But during surgery, his blood pressure dropped. The procedure couldn't be completed. He came out of surgery with an open drain from his stomach. They would attempt surgery again later.

He never recovered. Over two months, my mother would sit at the hospital day and night. Often, I would join her. My dad was alert most of the time. He would sit with an oxygen mask on his face reading his favorite newspapers. In lengthy discussions with my mother, they settled their affairs.

She knew he loved her before he died. He thanked her for being such a good wife in a heartfelt note on her birthday in early May. She now knew their finances. He spent those hours preparing her for his end and her future. He encouraged her to marry again. She was 52.

During this time, Allen opted to be airborne. Both the airborne units, the 101st and the 82nd, were out of Viet Nam. If you were in an airborne unit, it guaranteed you wouldn't go to Nam. Several weeks at jump school at Fort Benning in Georgia, then to Fort Bragg in North Carolina, the home of the 82nd airborne. I was to join him. He had rented an off-base trailer.

The day came to leave for North Carolina. I would leave at 2:00 a.m. by Greyhound for the airport in St. Louis. I would sit at the airport until early in the morning and fly to North Carolina with Nicholas. Before I could leave, one of those urgent and dreaded calls came from the hospital. Come to the hospital now. I went with my mother.

My father had a near-death experience. He saw himself leave his body. He saw the medical team frantically working on him. Soon he saw a river and was standing on the banks. He was joined by his friend, a Norwegian man from his earliest days in the United States. As quickly as he left his body, my father saw himself returning to the stark puke green hospital room. He saw the medical staff begin to relax their frantic activities.

Soon they told us that he was better and stable. We went home for some sleep. The next morning, a Sunday, he scolded my mother for not bringing the Sunday newspaper. One of my last memories of my father was that morning. I can see him with his eyeglasses perched over the oxygen mask, propped up in bed reading the Sunday paper we got from the gift shop.

The next day I went to North Carolina. Lambert Field, the airport in St Louis was deserted when I got off the bus with Nicholas in my arms. I went to the women's bathroom and sat on the couch there until it was time to go to the gate for my flight. I was scared and hiding out in the woman's bathroom seemed safe.

I arrived in Fayetteville by Piedmont Air. They lost my luggage, and it was never recovered. For weeks in the blistering heat, I wore my only item, a red wool jumper. Much to Allen's dismay, I would wear the jumper without a shirt as a sleeveless dress. I was violating the holiness code of sleeves in dresses.

It was necessary to find a church. The first one we went to was a large and unusually formal Assemblies of God. It seemed so odd that they only prayed in a prayer room. They had taken out the altar benches in the sanctuary.

The worship was very formal. That was the first time I heard a choir sing "hear our prayer oh Lord," after the pastoral prayer. Nothing wrong with that but they were supposed to be Pentecostal. To this day that is on the only Pentecostal church where I have ever heard that sung.

We wanted more lively worship. We wanted something that seemed more like home. We shopped around some and finally found a small independent Pentecostal church pastored by Marcus Borman. He and his wife Betsy provided transportation for us. Even though Betsy wore pants, and they watched television, Allen liked them. I convinced Allen we could have a television too. Soon I was wearing pants.

Early in June, the Red Cross notified Allen's commander that my dad was near death. Red Cross paid for our air tickets and off we went. We sat at my father's bedside for a week. He was unresponsive most of the time. He breathed his last on Sunday evening, June 13, 1971. I was there when he died.

I called the church my parents had been attending before he got sick, a start-up Assemblies of God church that met in a small house. Lon Calloway who sat with my mother day and night. He was always there. I remember seeing him sitting in a chair fast asleep while he waited with my mother outside my dad's hospital room. He mobilized a few people to take turns sitting with my mother. His wife Stella would take a shift and another minister, Brother Norris or his wife, would take another. Both the pastor of First Assembly and this pastor visited and prayed for my father.

Pastor Lon was there by the time my father was disconnected and the room tidied. My dad, my hero, the man who seemed to always cherish me was gone. Covered in white he seemed at peace. As we entered the room,

Lon led us in prayer as we joined hands as a family surrounding my father's body. It was hard. But I was in a bubble of denial. I would only understand the magnitude of my loss many years later. I was a nineteen-year-old orphan, with a child and another on the way, who's only ally was gone. Never would I hear him say *"Min Kjaere Ven"* the Norwegian pet name he had for me – 'My dear friend.'

My brother had come about a week before my father passed. Being the oldest, my brother took charge. I was considered too young and too female to be involved in the arrangements. The next day they took all my dad's clothes to a charity. It was too soon, too hard but my brother planned to leave right after the funeral. The rationale was that he didn't want to leave that for my mother to do alone. My brother took the most cherished item, my father's Bible, with him. I got nothing. A single grave plot was purchased. Much later, my mother would buy the plot next to him.

The funeral was officiated by both the pastors of our family's world. It was difficult for them. They didn't have a good relationship but they both did a wonderful job of honoring my dad. My other brother didn't come to the funeral. We shed a few tears and laid him in the ground to await the resurrection. Of my siblings, I am the only one who regularly visits that grave. I bring flowers and each time I understand increasingly how deep the pain of this loss is.

Allen and I went to North Carolina. My brother and family went back home to Canada. My mother grieved alone. She lived alone at 909 Wilkes Blvd. She worked part-time as a caregiver for older adults. How hard those days must have been for her!

As the weather began to cool, it was time for my baby to be born. I was seeing a doctor off the post. He was recommended by Betsy Borman. He wasn't very good. On October 6, 1971, I saw him for a routine visit. He said I was ready to have my baby. He told me to come to the hospital in the morning and be induced. It was likely a matter of convenience for the doctor. A holiday weekend was coming, Columbus Day. He didn't want his weekend interrupted for my baby's birth.

I tossed and turned all night. Soon I would find out whether my baby was a boy or a girl – would the name be Johanna or Justin Olav. I arrived at the hospital the next morning. I was taken to a labor room. There was another woman laboring in a bed next to me. Once settled, the doctor came in and broke my water. To ensure a quick delivery, I was given Pitocin tablets to put on my gums.

It worked quickly. I started strong contractions. I was in active labor for not more than an hour when I was whisked to the delivery room. There was a quick but unsuccessful attempt at an epidural. That process included harsh language from the doctor who kept asking me if I was sure I had one with my first child. Finally, they put a mask over my face and told me to breath in the gas. When I woke up, I had no baby.

I was told he was a boy. He was in the nursery. He wasn't doing well. He was small, 6 pounds and one ounce. Complications kept him in the hospital. Once again, I went home with empty arms. I think these experiences, compounded by the loss of my dad and the loneliness of Army life, made life with a newborn much harder.

Justin was a sweet, quiet, good-natured baby. But Justin was sick. We made many trips to the ER. He was in the hospital with bronchitis and pneumonia often. He was allergic to milk-based formula and would projectile vomit. At 9 months, he still wore 3-month size baby clothes. He wouldn't walk until he was 22 months of age. We never knew why. A hospital stay for evaluation and testing was scheduled.

During that time in the hospital, a doctor came into examine and asked questions. As he was examining Justin, he came to his diaper area. At the same time, the doctor decided to ask me about the physical attributes of the men in Allen's family. The doctor was asking about their stature. But since he had the diaper area completely exposed, I thought he was asking about Justin's "parts."

"*How big are your husband's brothers and father?*" he asked.

I blushed and stammered, "*I don't know, I've never seen them.*"

Only much later did I realize that wasn't what he was asking.

Justin was evaluated for cystic fibrosis. They told us how serious this was. Fortunately, that test was negative. After a few days, they discharged him with a vague diagnosis of "failure to thrive."

Military pay was regular, but it would disappear fast. Money was tight after the first week of the month. We would pawn an item, then retrieve it. In desperation for money, I got on the city bus. My childhood in Brooklyn made me proficient in bus travel. A short trip to downtown Fayetteville would take me to a seedy place where I could sell my blood for $15. That $15 bought a lot of food at the Winn-Dixie in those days.

Life was easy in many ways. It had a regular rhythm. I made friends with other Army wives. One nameless woman saw herself in me. She insisted that I learn to drive. She handed me her keys and said: "*you can drive my car at any time. And when you are ready, I'll take you for your license.*"

She had a nice car. I was too scared to drive it. But I did drive our red and white Rambler station wagon we owned. It had an automatic transmission instead of the tanklike 51 Chevy we previously owned. It wasn't hard to drive. Soon I got in the car with an MP on post. I took the driving test and passed on the second try. On the first try they said I ran a stop sign. I insisted I stopped but I guess I didn't stop long enough. There was nothing coming so I barely tapped the brake.

At 19, I finally had a driver's license. Freedom. No more begging for rides. Getting up early I'd drive Allen to post to keep the car for the day. Often, I'd be on post when they'd play the National Anthem over the loudspeakers. Every car would pull over and park. Every soldier saluted and stood at attention. The post was frozen in respect for the nation.

Marion, another neighbor, took me under her wing. I'd run in and out of her house for friendship, advice, and an occasional cup of sugar. I wanted Allen to reenlist. With a "re-up bonus," we could buy a double-wide trailer. He'd make Sergeant. We'd be set for life.

Justin's lack of development was not our only major problem. Because Justin was quiet, Allen never abused him like he did Nicholas. Nicholas was already being beaten by the belt for minor infractions. The Bible said to spare the rod was to spoil the child.

The Borman's, the pastors of the small church we attended, helped us from time to time. We spent a lot of time with them, in their home, with their children. It was a warm weekday morning. Brother Borman came to my door. Only the screen was closed, and it didn't have a lock. He knocked on the screen. When I didn't respond right away, he walked in.

By the time he came in, I had come to the living room of the trailer. I was holding Justin. He said he was there to pray for Justin. He said he was concerned for us. We sat down on the couch together to chat about Justin's health and development and the upcoming hospital stay. I expected him to anoint my son with oil for healing. We believed God healed. I was thankful for this visit.

A father of four, and a pastor, he seemed fatherly to me. I was accustomed to having a pastor involved closely in a family's life. While Justin didn't have a life-threatening condition, as a young mother, I was very concerned.

Brother Borman was dressed in work clothes. Without warning, he moved closer on the couch. He had no anointing oil in his hands. Without warning, he leaned close to kiss me saying "I see how you smile at me. I know you want me." He leaned closer kissing me hard on the mouth. He attempted to open my shirt grabbing my hand to his crotch.

In shock and horror, I pushed him away. He persisted. I resisted. I got up. He followed me. I walked toward the door. As he came closer, I ordered him out of the house. He resisted but eventually I got in a position where I was able to push him out the door. At that point he said, *"I'm sorry. I'm sorry."* He complained that in the struggle to get him out the door, he had ripped his pants.

As soon as he drove away, I ran to Marion. I told her what had happened. She told me to call Allen. I did. He asked me what I did. He asked me if I had done anything. He asked me if I had asked for it. Pleadingly, I told him NO to each of these questions.

Marion, wiser, was my advocate and support. She was shocked at Allen's behavior and responses. She encouraged me to stay with her until Allen came home. I had been at her house about an hour when Brother Borman returned. You could tell he had showered. His hair was slicked back with too much hair oil. He had changed into a pale blue leisure suit. Marion said, "Look, he wants to make a better impression." The thought of that scared me.

He knocked on the screen again. He went in the unlocked screen for a second time. I could hear him calling my name through the open windows. I could tell he was walking through the trailer searching for me. I was very thankful I had stayed with Marion.

Allen got permission to leave post. Before leaving post, Allen found Sister Borman who was a civilian employee. In anger, he asked her what was wrong with her husband. She knew. She didn't know it would be me. But she knew. She knew he had a problem. This was not the first time. When Allen came home, he again questioned me. It must be my fault. I must have done something.

That night, while I hid in the bedroom, Brother Borman came for the third time that day to the trailer. He came and apologized to Allen. He told him he was sorry. Allen accepted his apology. I was never offered an apology. Marcus took a tent and went to the mountains. He went to fast, pray, and repent. Once forgiven, he preached the next Sunday. How many other women were there? I'll never know but this was not the first trip in a tent and likely not the last

I lost a lot that day. I almost lost my faith that day. Months of struggle followed as I tried to reconcile how this man of faith, my pastor, would want to violate me. I wondered if it was my fault. Had I smiled too much at him? Allen believed I had done something to encourage him. Once again, his wayward wife needed to be controlled.

Betsy Borman never spoke to me again. She and her husband continued in ministry. Finally, confessing my sins and doubts, we looked for another church. We found a Church of God (Cleveland TN) on Cumberland Road. Ironically, now we looked too worldly to be holy. I was brought to the altar more than once to be saved and sanctified because of my clothing and hair. I also pierced my ears at that time.

Christian TV helped preserve my faith in that trailer. Yes, evil TV. Jim and Tammy Bakker were on TV with their children's show. This was long before their national popularity. Susy Moppet and the batting eyelashes of Tammy reminded me that faith was still out there.

Despite my protests and desire to stay, he took an "early-out" rather than a "re-up." I traveled back to 909 Wilkes Blvd. My mother bought her first home, a mobile home, and moved out. Allen joined me. We were back home, ready for the next chapter. A business, Lynch Custom Hay and Straw Services, an education at MU, suicide attempts, and abuse are the coming attractions.

TEN

Being a veteran and older, Allen was now creditworthy. Allen was ready to get a business loan and be an entrepreneur. He started with a used tractor, mower, rake, and baler. Soon he moved up to a brand-new blue Ford tractor. It didn't have a cab, but the summer heat of Missouri was not a problem for him.

I drove the red and white Rambler station wagon. He had a blue Chevy pick-up. With the boys in the car, I would travel the gravel roads to find the field where he was mowing. I would have a jug of tea, some sandwiches or left-over fried chicken. Often, I would get lost, as directions were always vague. Attempting to turn around, I'd end up in a ditch. Somehow, I always got out.

Then he found a flatbed drivable hay hauler. It was meant for the flat fields of Kansas, not the hills of Central Missouri. It was a novelty. We drove to St. Louis together to buy it. He returned driving this monster through St. Louis rush hour traffic with me dutifully following behind.

We went to farm auctions. I drove to a neighboring town where we banked regularly. I was so tired that at times I'd arrive at a destination not remembering how I got there.

We picked up a few employees. I think all of them eventually got paid. I did the record keeping and financial books. Allen would mow and rake. The men would help with the hauling. The conveyor belt on the hauler was to have eliminated this expense, but it didn't work.

I kept trying. I kept failing. Now I wanted to die. Twice, in desperation, I overdosed with pills. I was taken to the ER. They released me as a neurotic woman looking for attention. Allen yelled at me.

Next, I tried to run away. I was following a familiar pattern. I was going to go home. I was going back to Brooklyn. I had my two boys in the car. I even picked up two hitchhikers. Two young men with a sign about Jesus. I got in the station wagon and got about 50 miles outside of Columbia when the car broke down.

My hitchhiker friends were of no help and moved on. I walked to the closest exit ramp carrying Justin with Nicholas holding my hand. I couldn't do anything right. I called Allen. He came in the blue pickup truck. On the way home, he started screaming at me. I grabbed the door handle. Justin was still on my lap. At 70 miles per hour, I managed to open the car door. I was going to jump out. I was so desperate. I was such a failure. Allen grabbed the door as it swung open just in time to prevent my success. When I think of that day I shudder.

With the help of the GI Bill, Allen went to the University. I tried as well. I was admitted without a High School diploma for the summer session. I dropped out without doing proper documentation. Those F's still stand on my transcript. Ultimately, they prevented graduation with honors.

Allen took Greek to prepare for ministry. I helped him with the flashcards. He also found a social life. He started to drink. He started seeing other women. He started sleeping with them. I knew but I didn't want to believe it.

We moved to another house. We did without food as now money went not just for his clothes and tools, but alcohol. More than once I rode in terror on the gravel road to our house while he drove drunk. I would beg him to stop. He would backhand me and tell me to shut up.

On a Thursday morning, a woman named Bea knocked on our door. We were living in subdivision outside of Columbia. It was on a gravel road. About 40 houses lined the only street of this subdivision. Many of them were duplexes but ours was a single house near the end of this one long street. Our address was Rural Route 2.

I didn't know Bea. She was quite a bit older than I was. She went to the same church. She worked at a grocery store. I'd shaken hands with her a time or two at church and would greet her if she waited on me at the grocery store. I was surprised to see her.

I invited her in. We sat down on an orange couch. The couch faced the large window and, in the background, if you listened hard, you could hear Allen snoring in the bedroom. Even though it was the middle of the afternoon, he was in bed.

I told the boys to go play and surprisingly they listened. I was puzzled. She explained that she had been praying that morning. She said God told her that I had a need. God told her to find me and meet my need. I squirmed. I wondered how she found me.

She continued by saying she had called the church. It was pastor's day off and couldn't be reached. But he didn't know exactly where I lived so he wouldn't have been any help. His secretary offered my address. She told her Rural Route 2. That didn't help at all. Rural Route 2 encompassed several square miles.

So, what did Bea do? She got in the car, bowed her head, and said, "*Lord, you know where she lives. Give me directions.*" She said she'd get to an intersection and ask the Lord which way to go. She got to the subdivision. Now what? There were so many houses and no names on the mailboxes. She prayed again. She said my door was the first and only door she knocked on.

She kept pressing me about my need. Finally, I told her with great embarrassment that we needed food. When she asked where Allen was, it wasn't in an accusatory way. She just accepted that he was sleeping, and the reason didn't matter. I was nervous that he'd wake up and be mad that she was there. I prayed he'd stay asleep. He did.

She asked me to go to the grocery store with her and pick out the food. I declined because I was afraid. I was afraid I'd pick out too much food. Or she'd judge me for what I picked. I figured if God told her where I lived, He could help her pick out the food.

She left and about an hour later she returned. Brown paper grocery bags filled the kitchen. I remember she even thought we were worthy of a roast.

Eventually, he moved in with one of his girlfriends. I was unwanted and a failure once again. Maybe I deserved the abuse. He had a job at the Scottish Inn motel at the east end of the business loop as a night clerk. It was a low-budget hotel with dingy rooms and a small lobby. I would go there night after night and beg him to forgive me, to come home. I would sob and cry begging for forgiveness for whatever I had done. I never knew what I had done, but always assumed it was my fault.

In later years he would tell our sons that he left me because I didn't iron his blue jeans with a deep enough crease. Like not folding his underwear correctly, I became rebellious. I still don't think jeans should have a crease. Nevertheless, I would iron them. The fact that I could hand iron and hand starch Army fatigues with perfection a few years before was now forgotten.

I prayed and cried for a miracle. God knew where I was and what was going on. Yet, I frequently wondered whether it was deep sin in me, or did I deserve this?

Notwithstanding my prayers, it wasn't enough. He was gone. He never came back to that house. I was alone. I couldn't afford the rent. I moved in with my mother. I applied for welfare for the first time. Commodity foods again appeared on the table. I would be one of the first to receive food stamps when they went national in 1974.

I was very despondent. At one point, it was recommended that I become an inpatient at the local mental health facility. Allen found out and said he'd take the children. I changed my mind about becoming an inpatient or an out-patient at the mental health facility. I wasn't going to risk the boys going with him.

My mother urged me to put Nicholas and Justin in foster care. Her rationale was that I could get them back after I got my life together. I wouldn't do it. These were my children. I'd do whatever it took to keep them with me. I was now a single mother, another label, another stigma.

My mother pushed me to get a divorce. I found an attorney. The attorney filed. Allen never showed or contested. We were divorced. I continued to pray that God would restore our marriage. I knew that God wanted our marriage to survive. We had exchanged vows. I meant them. In my heart, I wasn't divorced. Redemption would come. I believed it. Our marriage would be saved. Unfortunately, that prayer was answered.

ELEVEN

*H*e came back. We remarried. My mother had married a man we had met in that first year in Columbia. A widower from the Church of God Holiness and my mother exchanged vows just before Christmas 1974. Allen and I were there when they said their "I do's."

My mother's hair started to grow, eventually reaching her waist. The woman who loved soap operas and game shows no longer watched TV. The same energy she used to learn to cook Norwegian food she used to cook country food to please her new husband. We merged as a family. I gained five siblings. Allen would not be with us for long. It ended quickly with more infidelity. It ended the day he beat me with the ice scraper.

Elizabeth Joy. Bethy Joy. A daughter. MY daughter. I couldn't hold her. I looked at her through the same panes of glass where I saw Nicholas for the first time. This time no scowling nurses. This time I could go into the NICU. If I scrubbed, wore a sterile gown, I could touch her. I scrubbed and scrubbed. I covered my hospital gown with a yellow isolation smock.

I reached my scrubbed hands into the portals of the Isolette. I could touch her. Would she live? I didn't know. I was afraid to hope. She was over 5 lbs., but still so tiny. Everyone spoke to me in tones that told me not to hope too much. No one could tell me whether she'd live or die.

Regularly they came to stick her with thin needles sucking the blood up in a syringe to measure her blood gases. They poked and prodded her with all manner of instruments, tubes, and needles. She had jaundice. With her little eyes covered, under the bilirubin light she went.

But I could touch her. They told me I could pump breast milk and bring it in for her use. I tried and tried but had little success with the pump. I know at least once they confused someone else's breast milk for mine and fed it to her. I didn't care. I just wanted her to stay alive.

While still in the hospital, Allen came to visit. His sister had told him he had a daughter. He strutted into the room with an attitude. He didn't ask me how I was doing. He didn't ask about the baby.

I told him I was naming her Elizabeth Joy. I told him she might die. He said nothing.

His only concern was to ask when I was filing for a divorce. I said I'm not – you can. Waiting in the lobby was his new girlfriend. He was only there to make it easier to marry her.

Certainly, he wanted to see his little girl who might die. I told him they would let him scrub in and touch her. He never visited Nicholas when he was in the same NICU. He hadn't changed. He said *"no, I don't want to see her."*

He left. I cried. What would become of us? My little family of four with no support, no job, no future. I cried a lot. In the back of my mind was, what can I do? What don't I know until I try? Try what?

My mother and her husband finally returned from their trip and came to see us. I remember her husband was particularly squeamish about all the needles. He seemed to have compassion for the poor little waif in the Isolette.

My mother was kind but a bit distant. I was still living free in her trailer. I did pay the utilities but often I ran out of money before they were paid. My welfare check was $150 a month and would go to $170 now that the baby was born. When the utilities were shut off for lack of payment, my mother would pay to have utilities turned on. She helped with food and often I went to her house to eat.

After a few days, for the third time, I left the hospital without a baby in my arms. I went to the welcoming home of Rebekah and David. My boys joined me. I was told I could stay as long as I wanted. I went daily with what little breast milk I managed to pump and would spend time with my new baby girl. I could hardly wait to hold her close.

There was more bad news. The pediatric cardiologist was called. Elizabeth had a heart condition. It might be serious, but it might not be. She might outgrow it, but she might not. If she didn't, when she was 2 or 3 years old, she'd have surgery. Finally, they let her go home with me.

The kind women of the church quickly threw a baby shower for me. I think the support of pillars in the church like Rebekah and David, gave me some renewed respectability. Or maybe it was because I just kept showing up. I kept going to church with my boys in tow. Boys who were often in trouble with someone. Boys that climbed in windows and ran too much. Occasionally they'd throw gravel in the parking lot. They were full of life and adventure.

Before there were diagnoses of ADHD you were told your child was hyperactive. Nicholas was diagnosed as such. They sent me to a social worker who told me I needed to be calmer, and a resident psychiatrist watched Nicholas draw and talked to him about life.

I stayed for several weeks with Rebekah and her family. All four of us found respite and love there. They prayed over us, fed us, loved us, and gave us immeasurable support. Finally, fearing I might wear out my welcome, I thought I should go home. One never knew what my active boys might do. After all, I was rejected all my life and one needed to be careful.

Back I went to my trailer home where I'd sit on an orange cushioned armchair trying to nurse my baby. I had not tried to breastfeed the other children. I struggled. I was determined. I had some peer support from some of the other young women at the church. But I struggled.

One night, I was desperate; I was frustrated and in tears. I wanted so badly to do what was best for my baby. I knew breastfeeding was best. But I couldn't get her to latch. Probably this was due to having been fed bottles in the hospital. Laying in my bed with Elizabeth in a port-a-crib on the other side of the room, I prayed. *God, if You want me to breastfeed this baby You must help me. I can't do this.* That night, I cried myself to sleep. Soon the newborn's cry of hunger at 2 a.m. woke me. That night and every day and night for the next 15 months, she latched on and ate and grew. She began to flourish.

TWELVE

C rescent Meadows was a large trailer court outside of Columbia in an area known as Prathersville. We lived in the "center" of this large trailer court. Many of the original people who moved into that trailer court owned the lot their trailer sat on. Other people rented their lot and lived in a trailer they owned. Still others simply rented the trailer from someone else who either rented or owned the lot.

Across the meadow, behind the trailer we lived in, was the Juvenile Detention Center for Boone County. In the bullseye of the center of the trailer court was a small office and a laundromat with a payphone. The payphone was my only access to making doctor's appointments or reporting an emergency.

There are two colors I think of when I think of that trailer. Blue because it was blue on the outside. Orange because of the furniture. It had been a base model and had no frills. The beds were hard. It had cheap wooden paneling throughout. A window air conditioner cooled the living room in the summer. The living room also had large windows which brought in a lot of light. It helped with the feelings of claustrophobia.

The two bedrooms were on opposite sides of the trailer. The one bathroom was near the back and the kitchen was in the middle. The kitchen also had a nice window over the sink. Throughout was a brown brick vinyl flooring. It had a main door that came into the living room. The back door had no steps. If you had an emergency, you had to jump the four feet to the ground.

Nicholas had the run of the neighborhood. He knew everyone. Often as the sun began to set, I would wonder where he and his little brother were. They could be anywhere in the maze of that trailer court. I had no idea where to start. I'd sit in the orange chair with Elizabeth and start to pray. *"God, please send Nicholas and Justin home."* Almost always, within a short time, they came through the door.

Nicholas was so proud of his baby sister. So was Justin but it was Nicholas who one day decided to show off his sister. I had been to the laundromat across the street in the trailer park. I walked in our front door to find Nicholas at the back door. It was open and in his arms was his tiny, beautiful baby sister. He was leaning outside the door showing her off to the neighborhood kids. Trying to stay calm, I was successful in retrieving her before an accident happened.

I was alone with three kids, but we were happy. I started doing macramé and decorated with hippie décor. I had a large collection of vinyl (records) in the new genre of Contemporary Christian music – the Jesus music. My favorite was Nancy Honeytree. I learned to crochet and made vests and floppy hats.

Nicholas kept bringing home dogs. We had several puppies that didn't survive. One, a beautiful little chocolate-colored puppy with blue eyes, got run over by the school bus. It had followed Nicholas to the bus stop.

Then Nicholas wanted a gerbil. We found someone giving them away. We called and picked up a gerbil. Immediately upon returning home, Nicholas held him. The gerbil bit him. Nicholas dropped it. We held its funeral. After lots of tears, we got another one. It survived for a while.

Then came Daisy. Daisy was an ugly female mutt. But she was a good dog. Daisy came into our family through a high school age girl we knew from church. For a brief time, she seemed to attach herself to our family. She, like most people, was looking for a place to belong.

She would spend time with Nicholas since she seemed to have the same level of energy. She heard about Nicholas's desire to have a dog. One day, she brought us Daisy. I wasn't happy but when your little boy looks at you with his bright beautiful big brown eyes and pleads to keep the dog, you say yes.

I had not grown up with a dog. I liked them but I was afraid of them. Family stories told me about a dog named Duke that we had when I was born. In addition to my parents not wanting another child, my brothers weren't happy with my arrival either. Perhaps we were always doomed to never have a relationship.

I was just learning to crawl. I was now down at Duke's level. Duke was a German Shepherd. He was big enough to have eaten me. He didn't want me around either! One night, while crawling on the floor I must have invaded Duke's territory just too much. He nipped at me. He went for my face. I screamed. The next day, Duke was gone.

This was why I was always uncomfortable around dogs. But here was Daisy. She followed Nicholas everywhere. They were best buds. Then the day came when she went into heat. Now, not ever having a dog or being around a dog, I had no idea what would happen. Every male dog in the neighborhood found its way to my trailer. I would let Daisy out and next thing a male dog would appear. One time I beat a dog off her. Daisy was exhausted.

Yes, you guessed it. We soon had a pregnant dog. I could barely feed my kids and the dog. But soon we'd have a litter of puppies. Daisy disappeared. We couldn't find her anywhere.

There was a nip in the air, and it was time to light the furnace. As I struggled with the match and gas, praying I wouldn't cause an explosion, I heard whimpering and dog sounds. Nicholas crawled under the trailer and there was Daisy with her seven pups. She willingly let Nicholas take the puppies out one by one to a waiting warm blanket. Once they were all retrieved, Daisy came out.

We kept one puppy. When they were weaned and able to leave, Nicholas sat on the steps of the Memorial Union at the University of Missouri with a box of puppies. A cute kid with a box of free puppies is hard to resist. After a few hours, all the puppies had a home.

I know we kept Daisy for as long as we could, but the time came for her to leave our family. I called the girl who gave her to me, and she took her. I hope Daisy and her puppy had a happy life. Over the years there were many dogs, cats, birds, hamsters, gerbils and occasionally a snake.

Life in the trailer court was hard but good. I applied to the University of Missouri again. This time, I had an "equivalency diploma", a GED. To my surprise, the University accepted me. I applied for financial aid.

Armed with grants and loans, three months after my tearful day watching graduating students from my hospital window, I was a freshman at the University of Missouri. A freshman not right out of high school but as a single mother with three kids. Maybe I wouldn't be a failure after all. I was ready to try.

Justin started head start. Nicholas changed schools several times because of moves or ways to manage my schedule. Elizabeth went to daycare on campus. Between classes, I would go to the daycare and breastfeed her.

First, I wanted to major in psychology. I took freshman psychology and found it boring. Then there was the issue of graduate school. I wasn't sure I could finish the bachelor's degree. I had three children. I was still on welfare. You major in psychology to get into graduate school in psychology.

Next, I wanted to major in Spanish. Then I realized that was unrealistic. Not only would I need a graduate degree, but I would also have to travel to a Spanish speaking country for a while. All language majors did that.

Then, I wanted to major in History. During my first year and a half, I accumulated credits that weren't needed for my ultimate degree since I couldn't decide what to do. I loved being on campus even though I was not like any of the other freshmen. I was moving toward the future.

Early that semester, I was visiting at my mother's house. When she first married my stepfather, they lived in a house that I remember as always being dark. It seemed it either didn't have enough windows, or they kept the blinds closed. I don't know. I know it was always dark in that house.

I started browsing through the local newspaper the *Columbia Missourian*. Tucked on the bottom of a page something caught my eye. It said: Lynch and Pickin Announce Engagement. Hmmm, was this a relative of Allen's? No, it was Allen.

A young girl, the same girl who waited in the lobby while he came and asked about divorce, was proudly announcing her engagement to Allen. She was from another town. Lived on a farm. It gave the name of her parents. It announced the date of the upcoming nuptials.

We weren't divorced. What to do? I've been told I'm "scrappy." I guess I am. I walked over to the wooden desk in the corner. I picked up a black rotary phone and dialed 555-1212. Without giving it a second thought, I called long-distance information and got the phone number of her parents. I dialed the number. A man answered. I asked, *"are you Mr. Bob Pickin?"* He said *"yes."*

I sighed and took a deep breath. My heart was racing. Anger had overtaken fear. I said, *"Sir, I'm not trying to cause trouble for you or anyone, but I am Allen Lynch's wife. We are still legally married. We have three children and the youngest is an infant. Before your daughter marries him, I thought you should know."*

Silence, long silence. *"What did you say your name was?"* I told him. I told him I didn't have a phone at home; that was true. I couldn't afford a phone. I gave him my mother's number and said goodbye.

First, I heard from Allen's mother. She told me that Mr. Pickin called her. She verified that I was indeed his wife and that we did have three children. Then I heard from him, and he said he wanted to meet me. I agreed.

I thought it best that the boys not be there. They stayed with the neighbor while I sat in the orange chair and waited for Mr. Pickin to come. I was nervous. What would they say? What would they ask? What should I say? I knew this was the right thing to do, because it was just wrong for Allen to be deceiving these people. I heard a truck door slam; I heard the familiar sound of someone walking up the metal steps that led to the front door. Mr. Pickin had arrived. With him was his wife and daughter, Laura Lee. Laura Lee kept wiping tears and blowing her nose. She seemed quite despondent. She was a victim too.

They sat on the couch; I sat in my orange chair clutching my fatherless newborn. He told me that Allen had said I was a tramp. He told them I had slept around and that the only child that was his was Nicholas. He said that Laura Lee knew he had a son but that he was divorced. It was clear that the parents knew nothing about his previous life. He was just a nice young man who loved farming.

Allen, always the opportunist, had found this girl from a farm while on campus. Before long he was driving her daddy's truck positioning himself to be the heir to the farm. Laura Lee continued to weep and wipe tears from her eyes. Mom sat in stone at times trying to console her daughter.

I looked at Mr. Pickin and said, *"none of that is true."* I was defensive. I was defending my honor and reputation. When I was done, he said, *"I can see you are a fine person and I'm sorry we put you through this."* Mom helped Laura Lee from the trailer. Mr. Pickin shook my hand and thanked me.

Their next stop was Allen's mother. They gave his mother the engagement ring that he had given Laura Lee. The engagement was called off. At least that's what the parents thought. Allen would continue to come to the house and ask about the divorce. At times, Laura Lee gave him money to file for the divorce. He gave it to me because I kept asking for child support.

Things were different for mothers trying to get child support from deadbeat dads in the late 1970s. But that didn't deter me. I would go to the county prosecutor's office and file a complaint. They'd find Allen and he'd sit in jail for a few days. Never got any money though.

Allen had just been released from jail. It was not long after the Laura Lee episode. I was sitting in my orange chair feeding Elizabeth one afternoon. The boys were out playing in the neighborhood. Boom, a loud sound came from the front bedroom.

When I went to investigate there was a bullet hole in the outside wall of the trailer that went over my sons' bed and lodged in the inside wall on the other side of their room. Had they been home, had they been sleeping on their bed, or had they been sitting on the bed playing GI Joe, they would have been shot.

Do I have proof it was Allen? No. But no one will convince me that it wasn't He was mad at being in jail. He was mad that I had ruined his engagement plans. He could have killed one of us. To this day I have PTSD reactions to startling loud noises.

I completed the first semester passing all my classes. A's and B's, it was Christmas time. Charity organizations helped us. The tree was up. It was a cold evening just before Christmas Day. There was a knock at the trailer door. It was Allen.

"What do you want?"

"I brought some Christmas presents for the kids." He handed me three small presents for the kids. They weren't wrapped. They were cheap but appropriate for their ages. I thanked him. He said *"wait! I have something for you."*

Shock and disbelief was my reaction. This was the guy that I really believed was going to kill us a few months before. He handed me a beautiful large jewelry box from a local jewelry store. I thought it odd. He left.

I was talking to his mother shortly after his visit. I tried to keep her in touch with her grandchildren. She started to laugh with that macabre laugh of hers. She said, "*you know where he got that jewelry box?*"

I said, "*no.*"

She said, "*Remember that ring he gave Laura Lee?*"

I said "*yes.*"

"*When he took it back to the jewelry store, they wouldn't give him his down payment back. They gave him a store credit. He bought that jewelry box with the store credit.*" It was my turn to laugh.

Several times Allen would come to my house, I would always confront him about child support. Sometimes he'd give me money. Sometimes that money had come from Laura Lee; money she had given him to file for a divorce. When their engagement finally ended, I don't know. I do know that he met another woman sometime after that. She would be Mrs. Allen Lynch for a very long time. Marriages that are long aren't necessarily happy.

I was faithful to church. I knew God was my only help. At times, because of residual guilt, shame, and despair, I'd wonder if God would help me. I had always been unwanted. I'd sit in that orange chair and listen to Nancy Honeytree sing *"I Am Your Servant."*

I'd cry and reconsecrate myself to the Lord. I was an oddity at church. There were not many single mothers, and they were not in church. Some people were incredibly good to me. Some, not so much.

I wasn't sure God loved me. When I was a kid, I kept getting "saved." Every time someone said, come to the altar and ask Jesus into your heart, I'd go. In many ways, I was still doing the same thing. Reaching out, but never assured that Jesus loved me. He just tolerated me because He was a good God. And even of which I was unsure.

One time I thought about the imagery of being in the palm of God's hand (Isaiah 49:6). I wondered where I was. I finally decided that I was hanging off the side of the thumb. I was barely hanging on. And maybe if I kept holding on, I wouldn't fall out of His hand. The thought that He would keep me in the palm of His hand was foreign to me.

I needed desperately a new and correct revelation of the *"overwhelming, never-ending, reckless love of God."* I continued to work and strive for salvation. It was free to everyone else but me. I could lead someone to Jesus and tell them that God is love. I could recite John 3:16 and believe that whosoever meant everyone. But the reality for me was, I couldn't grasp that I really was part of the whosoever and if I were at one time, I was now disqualified and needed to work my way back to salvation.

I connected with a girl I went to High School with. I hadn't known her in High School. Had I graduated, I would have graduated with her. She was also in the Hickman class of 1969. She started going to church where my family of four worshiped. She was a single woman and had a career. She and her roommate took a liking to me. We'd fellowship at times at her apartment or over food in a restaurant.

One time, she paid to take us all to Six Flags in St. Louis. Another time, she taught Nicholas to fish. It was his first-time fishing. She had an engaging laugh. She walked in the love of Jesus.

One day, she pulled me aside. She asked me to sit down. She told me that she and her roommate didn't think I should be living in a trailer, outside of town, with no phone in my trailer. She said you have three small children, including a baby. You need a phone.

Then she said, *"we have decided and have arranged for a phone to be installed. You can only make local calls. We will pay for it for the next year. Then we will re-evaluate."* As I remember, they paid for the phone until I moved from the trailer. No longer would I have to depend on the payphone in the laundromat. If there was an emergency at night, I had a way to call for help.

Nearly 50 years later, I had the sad honor of conducting this beautiful woman's funeral. In the last 20 years of her life, we had reconnected. She still encouraged me. She would also tell me how proud she was of me. She was Jesus in flesh when I desperately needed it even in her last twenty years.

Life continued. Church on Sunday, Sunday night worship would include a pitcher of root beer and a pizza if I had money. Another girl I went to High School with and who had come back into my life would help with the cost of the pizza. Or she'd come to my house and "hang out." Life was hard, but it was also good. I had good friends. I was doing well in school.

THIRTEEN

I was only slightly older than those in my classes but in experience, I was ancient. I had seen a lot of life. I had experienced love and marriage. I had three children. I'd been divorced and remarried. Sometimes I blended in but once people knew I had kids, I no longer fit in. Fortunately, I didn't take many classes that required group projects. Most of my classes were large lecture classes.

I took Geography and barely made it through. I took Sociology. I liked that. I took Political Science and barely remember it. And I took Beginning Spanish even though I had it in Junior High, and High School. Obviously, I did well. All of it was a review.

I took Cultural Anthropology the first semester. Our project for the semester was to write a cultural ethnography. I chose to do my ethnography on La Leche League, an organization supporting breastfeeding. I needed all the support I could with breastfeeding. They met all the qualifications of a sub-group. Perfect match!

I remember the night I worked on the final draft of my ethnographic report. I had no desk. I couldn't afford babysitting to go to the library to write. After the kids were asleep, I'd fix a box of macaroni & cheese. Usually, it was a generic variety. Then I'd open a 2-liter bottle of Tab. The Tab gave me caffeine and the mac & cheese gave me carbs.

All night I worked on that paper. I had note cards. I had the syllabus. I had some data. I was ready. I worked all night. Working all night on papers became the only way to get my work done. Often, if the weather was acceptable and my paper was done, I would go outside and watch the sun come up. Then I'd go to bed for a few hours of sleep.

The biggest problem was I didn't have a typewriter. I sat and handwrote the ethnography on lined notebook paper. I double-spaced by skipping every other line. I only wrote on one side of the paper. It was the best I could do. Sometimes I would have to rewrite a page because I made an error. Many times, when I handwrote papers I wrote them twice – a first draft and a final. Fortunately, that dear teacher took pity on me as did others after her. I not only passed but I got a good grade!

The first summer at the University I went to summer school. If there was financial aid available to pay for it, I took classes. I really don't remember how I figured out financial aid before the standardized FAFSA forms. But I did. I'd stand in line at Jesse Hall for my check every semester. The "ladies" behind the barred windows in Jesse Hall were known for their bad attitudes and abrupt actions. You could stand in a line for an hour only to have the window close with a bang just before your turn. If you were lucky, you only went once. Often it took days and weeks of return trips before your check would come.

I went to the church's college service on Friday night. There were married students, so I wasn't the only one who had kids. I wasn't much younger than the college pastor. My kids came with me, and Nicholas became everyone's friend. He went on a few retreats with the college students without me. But I still didn't completely fit in.

Services were great – this was the Jesus Revolution time-period. We sang the Jesus music. We hopped and sang loudly, we raised our hands in worship, and loved each other. Many of the women moved into the "sister's house" and the men to the "brother's house." There were even three married couples that tried living together in common.

I was still in my mother's trailer. I was sitting in that same orange chair for the first few semesters. It was the fall semester of my second year at Mizzou when I had some time between classes. I saw someone I knew from church. She was a nice young woman who always was willing to chat with me. She was going to see her advisor across campus. I decided to walk with her.

We went to Lewis and Clark Hall, the home of the College of Practical and Vocational Technical Arts. She was majoring in Recreation and Park Administration. I thought that was a rather odd major.

While I waited for her, I picked up a small green information sheet. It said something like, do you like people? Do you like arts & crafts? Can you crochet or knit? Nothing about sports. Nothing about anything I couldn't do. I am very physically uncoordinated. But I could do all those things. Then it said, maybe Therapeutic Recreation is for you.

The pamphlet informed me that I could work in mental health, with older adults, with developmentally disabled, or hospitals. I had found my major! It seemed to combine so many things that I could do, and I wanted to help people. And this degree would give me employable skills with a bachelor's degree.

I quickly changed my major. I had a lot of wasted credits. I also had a lot of required classes yet to take. Nonetheless, I finished in three and a half years with the three kids. I'd battled poverty. I took my children to school and daycare. I moved to a better trailer and then to the projects to have more room for my family. And I fell in love.

One of my neighbors had a brother who would come to my trailer and hang around. One night he had some story about not being able to stay at his sister's house and wanted to spend the night with me. I told him he could, but he had to sleep on the couch. He was surprised. He probably thought I didn't mean it. I did. He slept on the couch; I slept with a knife under my pillow just in case he came to the bedroom. He stopped coming around.

My mother's insurance agent showed an interest in me. He came around to sell me insurance and just visit. One day we went for a ride. We headed west on I-70 crossing the Missouri River at Rocheport. He pulled into a rest stop.

We took a walk. I thought maybe he was really interested in me. Of course, he knew I had kids. He also knew I went to church, loved Jesus and had "standards." He got to the point.

He said, *"I like you. I'd like to spend more time with you. But if you aren't going to have sex with me, I will move on."*

I looked at him and said *"no, that's not happening."* He pressed me more. I thought about it, but I said no. Jesus was too important and I wanted to please Him more than anything. He drove me home and he never came back, not even to collect the insurance premium.

The second summer session between sophomore and junior years I was sitting in Brady Commons. Every day I was there. Studying or eating or just people watching. I liked to go to the Commons because it wasn't too isolated like the library. Plus, I could get some cheap food. Breakfast was the best deal. Two eggs with toast plus beverage were less than a dollar.

Before long, I knew who the regulars were. Campus in the summer was almost empty except for the international students. They didn't or couldn't go home. Like me, they also were trying to get finished. Most were graduate students. Many were from Iran.

This was before the fall of the Shah and these Iranian students would stand outside the library or other strategic places on campus. They covered their faces with brown paper bags and would chant, *"Down with the Shah."* Sometimes they were in competition with street preachers that would show up on campus from time to time.

There was one graduate student who came every day to Brady Commons. I had seen him at church. He came with a professor and sat in the front. I was in the back with my kids. We'd pass each other usually by the self-serve soda fountain. We'd nod or say hello. He always just got a drink and had to have a napkin even with just a drink. Seemed he also recognized me from church.

I had been watching him at church for a variety of reasons. One of those reasons was that I found him attractive. Of course, I was convinced I'd never find love again. I was damaged goods. And then, what about the church? Divorce was frowned upon and disqualified you for certain things in the church. Remarriage only compounded those problems.

One day I had my nose in a book. I don't remember what I was studying. That day I was really studying. The graduate student sat down on the other side of the booth. He asked if he could stay. I said *"yes."*

He told me his name and I shared mine. We talked for at least three hours. I learned where he was from. He learned about my kids. We talked about his major. I shared mine. We talked about his attendance at church. His English was decent. And being the daughter of an immigrant/foreigner, I was always interested in being kind to people who were guests or new to this country.

As we were ready to part, he told me that one of the foreign students' groups was showing an Indian movie with English subtitles at the Memorial Union on Saturday. He asked me if I wanted to go. I said, *"I'll have to see if I can find someone to watch my kids."* He said, *"bring them."*

I thought that sounded safe. This already was different than the other two men who had expressed interest in me. I was also interested in him. Many times, my children have been either a shield to hide behind, or a security blanket. Having them would keep me safe.

We met in the Union. I will never ever forget the sight of this skinny dark haired South Asian man sitting on a bench. He had a brown paper bag in his hand. He was just sitting there waiting for me with this bag.

I approached him with my two rambunctious boys carrying Elizabeth in my arms. A child in your arms really can be comforting when you're nervous. He handed me the brown paper bag. He said, *"this is for the kids."* Now the boys came to life! *"OPEN THE BAG MOM!!"*

I opened it and looked inside. It was candy. But it wasn't one candy bar, or one candy for each of them. No, there were three large bags of candy. A full bag for each of them. All I could think of was – *OMG are they going to be wired for the evening*. It was sweet but at that moment, I really didn't appreciate it.

We followed him to a small auditorium. I was still incredibly nervous. What have I gotten myself into? It was dark in the auditorium. The handful of people who were there turned with mixed reactions as we entered. They were all South Asian.

Nicholas and Justin had already been won over by the candy. He was now their new favorite person. They argued as to who would sit next to him. Elizabeth was on my lap. Soon she started making noise. Up and down, I went in and out, trying to keep her from disturbing the movie. I would peer through a tiny window in the door to read the subtitles. It was an EXCEPTIONALLY long movie and didn't have all the beauty of more recent "Bollywood" movies. I thought that movie would never end. But on those brief moments I sat next to him, he reached out and held my hand. I was falling in love.

As we got ready to leave, he asked me if I wanted to get some food. If I had understood how difficult money was for him, I would have declined. He wanted to take us to a restaurant that was a college hangout that I had never been to before that. As we were completing our meal at the *Heidelberg*, Nicholas says, *"can you come to our house?"* I wanted to choke him.

"Sure, if it is okay with your mother."

I said, *"I'd have to also drive you home, I don't live on campus."*

He said, *"That's fine."*

It was already late. I really didn't want to do it. But we piled into my VW bug and drove the few miles to my trailer home. Immediately, I returned him to his basement apartment on campus.

He had no transportation other than his feet so I would help get him to places including work. He delivered patient dinner trays at the University Hospital. One of my stepsisters knew him. She worked at the Hospital. She told me he had asked her out once. She wasn't interested but said he was genuinely nice.

To say we "dated" is not really a viable choice of words. We spent time together. We got to know each other better. The kids loved him. He had just gotten his driver's license in Missouri and said he drove before he came to the US. I let him drive my bug! That was not the best decision I ever made.

I have no idea how many times he stalled the manual transmission as he attempted to drive stick. He'd roll backwards and car horns would blare. He'd kill the engine and people would yell nasty things to him. And I'd just sit in the passenger seat and smile.

He'd miss important meetings or classes because Elizabeth would cry for him. He would not leave the car if she were crying for him. He missed study time but still managed to keep pursuing his doctoral degree. One semester he taught statistics as a Teacher's Assistant (TA).

I was working part-time (work study) at the Center for Research in Social Behavior on campus. I was working for a Social Gerontologist and his graduate student. Every so often, at usually the right time, someone would come along and see something in me that I did not see. They encouraged me to pursue admission to graduate school in Sociology. I was interested in gerontology. I wanted to work with older adults in some capacity.

I also typed reports and research for Dr. Habbi and Caroline. I became a proficient typist. This was my second work study job. Previously I had worked in the Art Department typing tests on ditto masters or processing employment time sheets for the nude models.

Sociology seemed a very logical progression from Therapeutic Recreation. I was getting close to finishing my bachelor's degree. It was a time of newness, change, and decisions.

Love was once again distracting me from going forward. I was scared, I was confused. Much to my children's dismay, I broke up with the graduate student. He persisted and I kept running away.

One night I decided to drive to a friend's house who lived near Fort Leonard Wood. I was driving a large Oldsmobile Vista Cruiser by this time. I slipped and slid all over the road in a massive snowstorm to get away from his persistence. What I didn't know was that he had snuck into my house. By this time, I was living in the projects and had a three-bedroom townhouse type apartment. He didn't know that I wasn't coming home until Sunday.

I got home to a long-handwritten note in my bedroom declaring his love for me. He had taken my Bible and found verses about having a wife. He was begging me. He wanted to get married. I determined to resist.

I had finally officially divorced Allen for the second time. I wanted him to file and pay for it this time but eventually contacted legal aid and got some help. I went to court by myself to finalize the divorce. I felt so empty and alone and yet I also knew I had accomplished an incredible amount of progress toward a future for my children and me.

Child support was ordered but it would be many, many years before I collected a penny. They also ordered a dollar a year in maintenance for me. The law student recommended this so that there would be an order on the books in case he came into money.

It was early February. It was a very snowy winter in 1978. Valentine's Day was around the corner. A foot of snow blanketed the city. The

University closed for the day. I was cooking in the kitchen. I was making homemade spaghetti sauce in an electric frying pan. The kids were playing. Around two in the afternoon there was a knock on my door.

In front of my door was a frozen graduate student. Coming from South Asia he had no experience with snow. I opened the door.

How did you get here?

I walked.

You what?

I knew everything was closed. No buses, etc. And yet, there he was. It was three miles from his door to mine. Not a difficult walk when the weather is good but with a foot of snow, it was monumental.

He came in. He had another brown paper bag. Again, there was candy. Three small Valentine hearts of candy for the kids. One large Valentine heart for me.

"Why did you do this?" I asked.

"I didn't want you to have Valentine's without candy! I stopped at the drug store to get these."

I melted. I tried not to show it.

What did he know of Valentine's Day?

In a few days it was Valentine's Day. I bought him a red shirt. We went to Kentucky Fried Chicken and started planning our wedding. I was smitten and he was likely afraid I'd run again. We would get married as soon as possible.

I went to a store on Broadway. The best store at the time, at least in my opinion, was Suzanne's. I never shopped there. It was too expensive. I found a white eyelet dress with drop shoulders. It was simple. It was white. It was on the clearance rack because it was from the previous summer. Not appropriate for February in Missouri weather.

Our colors would be blue and yellow. I got a yellow ribbon to tie around the empire waist of the dress. I decided I wanted a halo of babies breathe. My matron of honor balked but it was my wedding. We placed a small order for flowers. I would carry a single yellow rose. We ordered three yellow rose boutonnieres and some yellow pedals. Along with the flowers from Nowell's Grocery we ordered a two-tier wedding cake. All totaled it came to a whopping $50. On an income of $170 a month, which was a fortune.

The groom didn't own a suit. A trip to JCPenney resulted in an approved credit card and a three-piece light blue suit. Finally, we went to Lamb's Jewelry store to pick out rings. I wanted our rings to match. I also really wanted a diamond engagement ring. Allen and I had remarkably simple gold bands.

After much discussion and an offer to buy a set for me (engagement and band) but with a non-matching band for him, I chose the matching bands with engraved crosses encircling the band. The nice people at Lamb's gave us credit. The last thing they said was we will send you the bill. Months went by and that bill never came. We should have investigated but we were busy with life, and it drifted from our memory. We never paid for those rings.

With the JCPenney card we purchased dark blue suits for Nicholas and Justin. They looked so handsome. Elizabeth, who was almost 3 years old, wore a long blue floral dress with an apron over it. Eyelet ruffled over her shoulders tied our outfits together. She was also haloed with babies breathe.

On Saturday, February 25, 1978, at 2 p.m. at the Memorial Union where we had our first "date" we became Mr. and Mrs. We married in the A.P. Green Chapel. Nicholas lit the candles. Justin was the ring bearer. Elizabeth was the flower girl. They were so happy. We were all filled with such hope for the future. We each took a lit candle and used them to light one single candle symbolizing our union. Our guests included my mother and stepfather, some of my stepsisters, along with the same South Asians who watched the movie with us were there.

The cake from Nowell's was beautiful. I had picked it up that morning and carefully brought it to the place for the small reception. We had opted to skip the bride and groom on the top. Instead, we had a silver cross with two wedding rings at the place where the crossbars meet. The Union catered some hors d'oeuvres that were washed down by punch.

When it came time to feed each other cake the woman who was my matron of honor decided I needed to smash cake in his face. She literally took my hand and smashed it into his face. Not familiar with this custom he got incredibly angry and pushed cake in my face – HARD. This was the first time I realized that we would have cultural issues to overcome.

Part of the catering was the service of an employee to help serve the hors d'oeuvres. I remember her cleaning up and then standing looking at us. She just stood there. I was perplexed. We were done. I realized long after that she expected a tip.

Once again, we were promised that a bill would come in the mail. I knew the man who managed the food at the Union from church. Whether deliberately or by coincidence, that bill never came either.

Off we went to Lake of the Ozarks for one night. We were booked at Tan-Tar-A. It was cold. He was driving my Oldsmobile Vista Cruiser. It was automatic and he was a better driver. A guy on a scooter led us to our little villa. I remember how he stood waiting and waiting for his tip. He kept showing us things and we just wanted him to leave. Finally, he did leave, probably cursing us under his breath.

We headed back the next morning and went to church together that night. I remember the feeling of the gold band now on my finger. As I would raise my hands in worship that night, I wanted everyone to see that I had a ring on my finger. We hadn't told anyone in the church our plans.

A missionary to South Asia spoke that night. Many years later, on our 35th anniversary we were back in Columbia and the widow of that missionary was speaking.

I still needed to finish two more semesters. I was close. I had been granted dual enrollment as a graduate student. I was on the Dean's List semester after semester. I felt more complete. I felt less rejected. I was a married woman. But this is not a fairy tale.

Yes, I now had my *prince charming*, and I felt like a princess. I felt awakened to have been chosen. Had he come to rescue me? Fairy tales aren't real. Life is never a fairy tale.

Heartsick

Unrelenting disappointment leaves you heartsick.
(Proverbs 13:12a The MSG)

I've believed in fairy tales far too long
I've believed in hope;
I've believed in dreams
I've believed in working hard
I've believed dreams came true

I've dreamed I'd be loved and cherished
I've given when I had nothing to give
I've cried an ocean of tears
I've loved faithfully
I've loved completely
I've loved selflessly

There is no prince charming
Dreams don't come true
Hope disappoints
My heart is empty
The pain never ends
And tears never dry

FOURTEEN

*T*he new normal began. He vacated his tiny basement apartment. We lived together in the projects. For both of us, these projects were luxurious. We had three bedrooms and a bath and a half. The kitchen was huge. Neighbors minded their own business, and the location was convenient. It was a few miles to campus and other than parking on campus, it was ideal.

I still got some welfare checks and food stamps. He had his part-time job at the Medical Center. Every semester there would be some money left on our financial aid award after tuition and fees were paid. We were happy and the kids were ecstatic to have a "dad." They started calling him dad immediately and started using his last name.

At the church, people were shocked. Some were happy for us. Most were skeptical. Others were critical. Several people in the church had befriended him before I met him. A poultry professor who was his first advisor was kind and interested. He was the one who first brought him to church.

Another man, Brother Edward sold paint at the Sherwin Williams store while leading an international student's ministry. Edward always greeted him with a big *Hallelujah Brother*. He had been a guest in Edward's house several times. Fondly, he still talks about how Edward's daughter tried to teach him to ice skate.

People who knew me had a little bit of caution but kept any concerns they had to themselves or brought it to God in prayer. Not so with Edward. Shortly after we were married, he said he wanted to talk to us before we left church on a Sunday morning. The kids were running around somewhere. Edward found a vacant office. We sat down. I barely knew Edward at the time. Edward's youngest son often got in trouble with Nicholas, but I didn't know Edward.

He sat behind the desk even though it was not his office. He glared at us shaking his head. My husband was the first to be addressed. He said, *"You are a phony. You only married her to stay in this country."*

I was shocked. The tension was palpable. He continued as he looked at me and said, *"And I don't know you very well, but you are divorced so you can be worth much of anything either."*

I do not remember anything else about that conversation because I shut down. It was a bruising conversation. For me, it was yet another reminder that I really was trash. I had been unwanted for a reason. Nothing I could do would ever make it right. Not even all the trips to the altar and all the prayers would do anything for me. I felt cursed.

Nevertheless, life in church had taught me one important thing. I knew that you can never equate Jesus with some of His people. Not everyone who names the name of Jesus lives like Jesus or acts like Jesus. Despite the bruising, I was not going anywhere. I was like Peter in John 6:67-68

> …Simon Peter replied, "Lord, to whom
> would we go? You have the words of eternal
> life. We believe and know that You are the
> Holy One of God."

While I was cursed, I was determined to stick around because I knew Jesus was the only answer.

It was summer of 1978 and I had just a few requirements to finish including my practicum. I found a placement at Boone County Hospital as a student intern in Recreation Therapy. I would work in their psychiatric ward. It was a small unit. The patients included chronic schizophrenic and other serious mental illness. The unit treated depression and alcohol and drug patients as well. We went to the movies, played games, made crafts and I learned how to chart. I like it. It was easy. On one therapeutic outing that summer, I took a female patient to the movies. We saw *Grease* together.

It was time for my last semester for the bachelors and my first semester in graduate school for Sociology. It was not a hard semester academically, but it was a hard semester personally. Marriage is never easy. And we had cultural differences. Our first major fight was over a washer and dryer.

While I loved that townhouse apartment in the projects, my husband did not. He convinced my mother and stepfather to rent a duplex apartment to us in the small town of Hallsville Missouri. They liked the arrangement because we were approved for Section 8 housing. This meant they would get a rent check from the government.

We were now fifteen miles from campus. Nicholas and Justin attended Hallsville Elementary. They walked to school in the morning. Because of subsidies, Elizabeth attended the local Montessori daycare. Every morning I would put canned refrigerator biscuits in the oven while we got ready to go to campus. When the biscuits were ready, I quickly spread some butter on each one throwing them into a brown paper lunch bag.

By this time, he had convinced another foreign student to buy his Mercury Monterey, and this was our transportation. Elizabeth would sit on the drop-down arm rest between us. While she would sing songs much to his annoyance, I would open the bag with the biscuits. We would eat all the biscuits as we traveled Route B into Columbia and eventually campus. In the summer he would drive with the window up even though we had no air conditioning. Roasting, I hung my head out the open window and panted for air like a dog.

After finding parking, we separated for our classes. One day, I had some time on my hand. I was having a challenging time keeping up with the laundry at home as there was not a laundromat close by. I took a trip to JCPenney's. While there I lusted over the shiny white washers and dryers. The sign said, "for $15 a month you can own these."

Certainly, we could afford $15 a month. But that credit card was not in my name. The salesperson approached me. I had lousy credit, but I had a ring on my finger. It seems odd now, but the rules about credit must have been different. The salesman eager for a sale, and me eager for a way to do laundry had a magical exchange. By the time I left the store I was able to buy the shiny pair with a signature as the wife of the credit card holder. Delivery to Hallsville would be in a few days.

It seemed like a wonderful idea to me. I was his wife. And we needed it. It was much cheaper to be able to do laundry at home. This would save money! It was brilliant.

He did not share my view. He got incredibly angry. I do not remember who said what. This was our first big argument. I remember screaming and a lot of crying. I cried hysterically. It touched off something in me that was unrelated to the actual event.

I do remember he accused me of motives I didn't have and was very harsh in his judgment. This touched off the feeling of always being wrong. My motives were judged. I remember a hellish drive into Columbia, and no one ate any biscuits.

The first big argument in a marriage is usually a jolt into reality. It is the first time you understand that life is not a fairy tale. Nevertheless, we survived. We had pledged to stay together for better or worse and we meant it.

As summer turned to early fall, I realized I was pregnant. I cannot say that any of my children were "planned." They were all loved and wanted from the first knowledge of their existence. After Elizabeth was born, I was sure she would be my last child. Now another child was on the way.

December of 1978, three and half years since that fateful moment at the hospital window, I would be a college graduate. However, there would be no pomp and circumstance, no cap and gown, no "real" graduation ceremony. I hadn't had a high school graduation and I would be denied a college graduation. Each department had their own small ceremony minus the trappings. I was wearing maternity clothes by this time. I selected a blossomy maternity smock to cover my belly. I wore a skirt with a hole for my belly.

My sons squirmed and fidgeted. Elizabeth was quietly sitting on her grandmother's lap. I heard my name. Because of my growing belly, it took a minute to gain my balance and walk to the front. It seemed so anti-climactic. Yet, I was now a college graduate!

There was an issue of art credit. It was the last humanities credit I needed. I had not been able to get to campus for the final because of snow. The chair of the department said, "*no problem. I will take care of it.*" That was the benefit of a small department. He took care of the requirement, but the F still stands on my transcript. It also prevented graduation with honors.

My attention turned away from graduate school to getting a job to support us. I hid the physical signs of my pregnancy and got a job at the Medical Center. I worked in purchasing for the labs first. I would call and place orders for chemicals and test strips. It was boring but it was work. In those days, a decent job at the Medical Center was considered quite a blessing. As my stomach grew, I saw the opportunity to get a job in the Medical School Dean's office.

Not knowing I was pregnant they hired me as a receptionist for that office and the personal secretary for the administrative dean. That was the Dean without a medical degree or PhD. He had an MBA degree and offered other skills. This was a very respectable job.

My husband continued to deliver trays at the same hospital. More early morning trips on Route B with a brown paper bag of biscuits. We knew we had only a few minutes to go when we would hear the familiar jingle on KFRU radio:

The jingle meant it was 7:55 a.m. A trivia question would be asked. Listeners would call in. If you were the first one with the correct answer you won a prize. Often, I knew the answer. Sometimes I would call but not be the first – one time I had the magic combination of the correct answer and the first to call. My prize was a three-piece chicken meal from KFC.

The day came when I could not hide my pregnancy any longer. My supervisor, the administrative dean, was incredibly angry. I gave my notice a few weeks before my due date. I decided to try to stay at home. I did not like the idea of someone else caring for our child. It had been a necessity with Elizabeth, but it did not have to be now.

May 3rd was my mother's birthday. She was disgruntled with me at the time. Throughout her life she grew to care for me in ways she had not when I was a child but there was always tension. On May 3rd, the women of the church threw a baby shower. This was a private unsanctioned baby shower. Official showers were for the first-born child only. The woman who hosted it did not know me, but she knew my friend who wanted to bless me with a shower.

I came home from the baby shower. I called my mother, and we talked about how this baby was not going to come on her birthday. She replied, "*you do have a few hours.*"

Hubby and I were both hungry. I fried two hamburgers. We sat on the couch watching Johnny Carson while we ate. I got ready to go to bed and he went to the couch. He had taken to sleeping on the couch because of the pregnancy, not because of problems between us.

First stop was the bathroom. I brushed my teeth and hair. I peed, washed my hands, and went to bed. I drifted off to sleep only to be awakened because I was soaking wet. Could my water have broken? I still had time to go before my due date. I knew my bladder was empty.

I went to the living room and announced that my water broke but I was not going to the hospital. He woke up immediately. I was shaking violently. I knew that meant I was in transition. The baby would come very soon. I thought it better to give birth at home than in the front seat of a Mercury Monterrey.

He dressed, got the car keys, and called my mother. She told him to drop off the kids at her house on the way to the hospital. He said, "*No Mommy, you must come here. There is no time.*" Somehow, he could call her Mommy even though I was told when I was young to not call her mommy anymore. She remained "Mother" to me until the day she died. We passed her car on Route B as she hurried to our house and we to the hospital.

On the way I insisted he stop. He would not. I was laying across the front seat. I had the urge to bite something. He gave me his hand to bite. Trying to reassure me that he could manage anything, he told me that he helped a goat give birth one time. That didn't ease my fears.

We arrived at the Medical Center. Everything moved in lightning speed and within thirty minutes a beautiful healthy seven plus pound daughter was born. My husband was in the room because he had attended Lamaze classes with me. This was something quite advanced for a guy from South Asia. Things moved so fast we never used the Lamaze method. Besides, he did not pay attention in class.

For the first time I left a hospital with a baby in my arms. There would be no trips back and forth to stare at a child through glass. I was home before supper the same day she was born. A friend brought a meal for us, and someone brought us food every day for a week or two. Our daughter was healthy and loved by both parents.

She took to breastfeeding like a pro. Her siblings were ecstatic. One day I found four-year-old Elizabeth lying beside her in the crib. We had good friends, a growing family, and tremendous love. Culture still presented issues at times. Especially when his brother came to visit.

His brother is a very talkative jovial person. I took to him immediately. He took over the boy's room and they slept on the couch. He called me "*bhabi*." I was told it is a term of respect. I have never been convinced of that. All the other sisters-in-law are called "Sister." Didn't they deserve the same respect I supposedly had? He was with us for several weeks.

My older brother, the perfect one, also came for a visit. I hosted a picnic at the Hallsville Park. Both our brothers, my stepsisters, my mother, and stepfather all joined together for spicy Asian food, hamburgers, hot dogs, and potato salad. It was a very pleasant multicultural day.

We took sight-seeing trips. We visited the Arch in St. Louis. We went to Worlds of Fun Amusement Park in Kansas City. Nicholas was thrilled that his new Uncle was willing to go on rides that neither of his parents would even consider.

One afternoon I was going to go the fifteen miles to Columbia. We had a small grocery store, Bummy's Market, in Hallsville. I do not know what I needed that day. To my surprise, Daddy decided to watch his baby daughter while I went shopping. I thought, GREAT! I muttered some instructions about the diapers.

After several hours, the time I really needed to shop and travel back and forth, I returned to find a screaming baby who smelled bad and an incredibly angry Daddy. His brother was sitting beside him with an equally stern look.

What took you so long?
You said you would watch her.

She pooped.
I know, I can smell it.
Why didn't you just change her?
I don't change diapers.

The implication was that in his culture, men do not change diapers. The look on my brothers-in-law's face told me he agreed. I took the poor child and changed her poopy diaper. The rule about not changing diapers never changed. None of our five children ever had a diaper changed by their Daddy. He is still proud of that.

I impressed my brother-in-law with my abilities in the kitchen. He did not expect to find homemade rotis at my house. He told me I could teach his wife to cook. Many years later, I was at his house and his wife was watching me cook in her primitive kitchen. I was preparing a chicken that was alive just minutes before. She watched me as I cut it into pieces like KFC would. I breaded and fried it. She kept saying "*No, you boil it.*" I would reply, "*No you fry it.*" She was right. That was the toughest old bird I ever tried to eat. It had to be thrown out.

I cooked a feast twice a day while his brother was there. Breakfast and supper were culinary events. One evening as I waited and waited for them to return to eat the feast I had prepared, he called from a payphone. I was informed that they had eaten at the mall. His brother needed something at the mall, and they were hungry. To that I replied, "*so what do you want me to do with all this 'shit?*'" His brother heard that remark. I was back down to the bottom of the approval list. How dare I call their food "*shit.*"

Notwithstanding the cultural clashes we were moving forward. He had two jobs now. He still delivered trays in the hospital. He also taught part-time at a vocational technical school in Mexico Missouri. He would take the brown bag of biscuits with him in the morning. After teaching all morning to rowdy disrespectful agriculture students, he would stop in Hallsville for a quick lunch. Usually, it was pita bread filled with a vegetable dish or potatoes to take in the car. He would eat supper at home arriving around 7:30 p.m.

His dissertation research completed and tabulated, it was time to draft the written dissertation. I had a new job. For hours, days, and weeks I sat at the typewriter we had rented, typing the dissertation. By now, I was a proficient typist. However, there was no spell check and corrections meant either retyping, or other white out tricks. Often a correction on one page meant everything else in the chapter had to be re-typed.

He took the completed work to his advisor. I hated his advisor. His advisor made massive amounts of work for me. Most annoying and challenging were the multiple pages of tables. Tables were an arduous task on a typewriter. At the completion and final approval of the dissertation, my reward was a movie trip to see Disney's *Jungle Book* and an electric blender to help make baby food.

With the school year over, new opportunities were pursued. He had a teaching license and was almost done with his doctoral degree. I was a homemaker. It now became my task to help him write a resume and get another job.

The pleasantness of Hallsville was about to be replaced with a new adventure. We prepared to move to Hannibal Missouri.

FIFTEEN

*H*e got a job! A full-time job with regular pay and benefits. Life was sure to change. We could get off welfare. No more visits to the welfare office or to get commodity foods. We would not live in section 8 housing. Being a teacher was a respectable job. And it paid a whopping $20,000 a year.

One Sunday we drove to Hannibal with our youngest daughter. We were smart. People didn't like renting to large families. We had four children. The landlord was thrilled to have a young couple with a baby rent his lovely and newly decorated small Victorian house. We were thrilled to find a rental for $150 a month. And the address was perfect, 2007 Grace Street. Grace, Grace! Amazing Grace, oh how sweet the sound!

They never asked if we had more children. We never shared that information. We signed the lease. I dreamed of being able to decorate the house. Mostly I dreamed of respectability. No one needed to know that I had never been wanted. No one needed to know I had been on welfare. We were relative newlyweds with college degrees.

Our marriage was okay, but marriage always needs strengthening. I thought this might do it. A fresh start in a lovely town made famous by Mark Twain. We packed our belongings and moved. I left behind the washer and dryer because this house came with one. It was in the downstairs bathroom, and they worked.

The front door had a large oval glass window. Hannibal is full of large and small Victorians. This one was small, but it had a majestic staircase. The kids soon discovered how fun it would be to put a crib mattress at the top and slide down the stairs. The stairs were a hit.

The large living room had huge windows. It was separated from the foyer by pocket doors which reminded me of the house I lived in as a child in Brooklyn. The time soon came that the boys would climb the sides of those doors to climb the walls. Their silly Dad would offer to pay them if they could literally climb the walls. They'd get to the top and exclaim "Look Dad." None of the kids had many memories of Allen. There new dad provided for them and got them into mischief.

In addition, he encouraged them to drink raw eggs as Sylvester Stallone did in *Rocky*. It was great amusement for him and great annoyance for me. The dining room which we never used as a dining room was also more than ample. The table we had was not beautiful enough to put in that large dining room, so it filled the kitchen.

The large kitchen and the half bathroom completed the first floor. The door to the basement stairs opened from the kitchen. We rarely went into the basement. The kids said they saw things in the basement and while that is easy to dismiss as childish, I know there were "things" in that house. Throughout the time we lived there I would often go room to room reading a scripture, anointing the room with oil, and pray. It may have helped but problems existed throughout our time there.

The house had three bedrooms upstairs. The boys would share a large room. The girls would share a small room. The baby, now a toddler, slept with us most of the time in the primary bedroom. We all shared the one full bath upstairs. There was no air conditioning.

Shortly after we moved in, I saw an ad in the local paper for a psychiatric assistant for the Partial Hospitalization Program (PHP) at Mark Twain Mental Health (MTMH). MTMH was housed in the local Catholic hospital one block down a steep hill from 2007 Grace Street. I applied and got the job. I would get $7000 a year to work full time. My duties were to collaborate with the director of the PHP program in group therapy. I would also assist the Recreation Therapist with outings to the bowling alley, parks, and crafts, etc.

I was so excited! My first "professional" job. We might make it to middle-class. Certainly, we were now respectable. I enrolled the school age children in the local Christian school at the Assembly of God church. Elizabeth started kindergarten. She memorized chapters of the Bible. I can still see her blonde pigtails and brown eyes light up as she would recite Psalm 8 in perfect King James English:

> O LORD, our Lord, how excellent is thy name in all the earth! who hast set thy glory above the heavens.[2] Out of the mouth of babes and sucklings hast thou ordained strength because of thine enemies, that thou mightest still the enemy and the avenger.[3] When I consider thy heavens, the work of thy fingers, the moon and the stars, which thou hast ordained;[4] What is man, that thou art mindful of him? and the son of man, that thou visitest him?[5] For thou hast made him a little lower than the angels, and hast crowned him with glory and honour.[6] Thou madest him to have dominion over the

works of thy hands; thou hast put all things under his feet:[7] All sheep and oxen, yea, and the beasts of the field,[8] The fowl of the air, and the fish of the sea, and whatsoever passeth through the paths of the seas.[9] O LORD our Lord, how excellent is thy name in all the earth!

The boys never excelled in the monthly memorization activities.

The baby went to the daycare program at same church. Donna was her teacher and would become a very dear friend. Her daughter Sarah was slightly older than our daughter. When I'd pick her up at the end of the day, she and Sarah were always together. We had such high hopes for Hannibal. Soon, I was pregnant again.

I loved my job. Glenn, my boss, was a free spirit. He had a beard he loved to stroke. It made him look like a therapist. He liked to talk about when the 'revolution' would come and quoted Saul Alinsky's *Rules for Radicals*.

I still quote Glenn from time to time. He would say things like, "*You know you are a grown up when you forgive your parents for their mistakes. They all made them.*" He was good at his craft and would bring people to a needed cathartic moment. Just before they would start to cry, he would ask them who do you feel most comfortable with. Often it was me. The patient would move next to me and before long, my shirt was stained with mascara.

He also like to help people with their anger issues. Out would come the *batacka bats*. They were long cushioned bats used for hitting. Often, I was picked for one of these sessions. The rule was, no hitting the head of your opponent. I got hit more than once in the head. Some people were holding a lot of anger. I had no idea how much anger I was holding.

Weekly trips to the bowling alley meant a trip to a neighboring town on a Tuesday morning. A mixture of PHP and in-patients would pile in the van for the short trip. They had the bowling alley to themselves. In the PHP program, we often had chronic patients in the program for months. One woman loved to bring change for the Juke Box. As we bowled, she jammed to *Elvira* by the Oak Ridge Boys. Every time I hear that song, I think of her.

As I grew with the job, I had a small caseload of my own. Occasionally we'd have high school age patients in the PHP. There were no specialized services for youth in the Hannibal area.

Diane was a beautiful girl. She had long wavy blonde hair. She came from a well-to-do family. She was very smart; her future looked so bright. She was clinically depressed.

In therapy she told of finding her aunt hanging from the basement ceiling. The woman had hung herself and Diane, still a small child had found her. Her cathartic moment came leaning on my shoulder as a dam burst forth into tears.

It was 1981 and she needed two electives to graduate high school. Not surprisingly she chose Psychology and Sociology. I was offered the job of homebound tutoring. I met her on Saturday morning. I was paid by the school board. Diane did well. She was preparing for college. In January of 1982, she also hung herself in the basement.

Coming that close to a family who lost a beloved daughter to suicide, I wondered, how would my family have reacted. Thoughts of suicide were mostly gone because I had children. I was determined to be there for them. They needed me. And their eyes and hugs told me they loved me. The time would come many years later when I convinced myself that my children would be better if I were dead. When that time came that I was convinced they would be better off without me, I would hoard pills for the time I'd be brave enough to take them.

For this new pregnancy, I decided to have the baby in Columbia. I had insurance and didn't have to go to a "clinic." I wanted to go to the "best" doctor in Columbia. Monthly I would drive the two hours to Columbia and two hours back. We also took frequent trips to Columbia to visit my mother. The trip was easy. We knew every back road and every place that would let you use the bathroom on the way.

One morning the phone rang. I grabbed it from the kitchen wall and started walking around the room as we were trying to get everyone out in the morning. It was my mother. My stepfather had died suddenly. It was December and it was very cold. We gathered to weep and cry and prayed. My children had no memories of my father. This was the only grandfather they knew. They took it particularly hard.

My mother amazed me. It had not been that long ago when she stoically stood by my father's casket. Now she was standing beside another casket. I watched as she greeted each person like they were guests in her home. She would walk with them up to the casket and share moments with each guest. My stepfather was well known in the community.

I remember he was buried with a hymnbook. The family liked the look of it because it had a cross on the front. It was also very fitting. He loved to "make music" and played hymns on his mandolin or banjo. Their church was wonderful. We feasted as a family at the church. When my mother died, even after 20 years of absence from that church, the church honored our family with another funeral meal.

His mother was still living and was devastated. This was now the second child who preceded her in death. Granny Ida was a beautiful person who was the only grandmother type person in my life. I cannot say I was close to her, but I could always sense her warmth.

Within a brief time, Justin was sick. He had extreme stomach pains. He was admitted to the hospital. He was probed and prodded. A surgeon was called in. Maybe it was appendicitis. No answers.

From his bed, he discovered that he could push that magic call button. Pressing it summoned a kind nurse who would get popsicles or Jell-O. Video games were also available by pushing the call button. The TV remote was also close. Eventually it was decided that maybe he was just grieving the loss of his grandfather and that is what caused the pain.

Next my blood pressure shot up. I traveled to Columbia to be hospitalized. It came under control for a short while and shot up again. I was in my seventh month of pregnancy. The doctor ordered me to leave work. Fortunately, I could take a leave with the guarantee of a job when I returned.

I moved in with my mother. She was newly widowed, so it was a good arrangement. I had our youngest daughter with me. She was now a year and a half. The rest of the family stayed in Hannibal and as soon as everyone was out of school on Friday, they would head to Columbia for the weekend. This went on for a few months.

It was May. Two years before I had given birth to a beautiful girl. Six years before in May I had stood crying at that window. Soon we would welcome our second child and my fifth child. I rested as much as I could while I waited to find out if it were a boy or a girl.

My blood pressure rose dangerously high again. The doctor told me to meet him at the hospital at 11:00 p.m. This gave time for my husband to arrive. Once in the hospital, they broke my water. Contractions started and by 1:30 a.m. a beautiful dark-haired little girl was born. The doctor had my husband assist in the delivery and he cut the umbilical cord. I held her briefly while shivering under a warm blanket.

I walked out of the delivery room to see our precious child in the nursery. This doctor was wonderful. Her delivery and my recovery were the easiest of all the children. We were now a family of 7. Time came to go back to work at the Mental Health Center.

I had been given a promotion. The Recreation Therapist had quit, and I was offered the position. I had free access to all the craft supplies. I would practice crafts so that I could teach them. I started doing "tole painting." Everything I owned was soon decorated with flowers.

Our baby girl was sick a lot those first few months. She had projectile vomiting. Breastmilk agreed with her, and I pumped. Nevertheless, she also had to be supplemented. She was hospitalized several times with bronchitis and pneumonia. I slept by her bedside in the hospital and walked upstairs in the morning to go to work. They evaluated her for Cystic Fibrosis and fortunately, it was negative.

Once again, we dealt with sickness. Nicholas and Justin both were sick. They had a terrible cough. Walking into the hospital ER, on a cold Sunday, it sounded like twin seals were calling to each other. They coughed in concert. They took turns coughing as if to outdo the other. We were well known to the ER staff. Every few months we were there for something.

Both boys were admitted to the hospital. I think when it started, they were sick. But they both discovered how wonderful that call button was by the bedside. They were treated for their cough. The pediatrician visited them regularly.

After a week of popsicles, video games, TV, Jell-O, and pudding, the doctor was concerned that they weren't getting better. He decided that maybe they needed an injection with an antibiotic. For some reason, they thought Nicholas needed it more. Being older, perhaps his cough was more convincing.

I was called and told of the plan. I thought hmm, this won't be good. About 5 minutes passed and I heard the hospital intercom say, "*Dr. Strong to the 1st Floor pediatric unit.*" Having worked in the hospital and with the in-patients on the Psych Ward, I knew what that meant. It meant they needed strong assistance to subdue someone. All the males I worked with ran down the stairs with me. Someone needed to be subdued.

Nicholas protested the shot. Nicholas was nowhere to be found. Staff started searching the hospital. My boss and I climbed in his little Honda and started the search. In retrospect, it seems unusual that no police were called to aid in the search for a sick child leaving the hospital.

Eventually we found him behind our house. He was scared. He also knew he was in trouble.

At the time I was so annoyed that I didn't think the situation through. I should have been understanding. I should have talked reasonably to him. Instead, I took him back to the hospital.

The waiting doctor told me to take both boys home immediately. He added, "*I never want to see you or any of your children ever again.*" Now we had no pediatrician. Again, not being understanding, I took Nicholas to school that very day. It was a decision that marked the beginning of the end of my relationship with that school and the church I attended.

I called another pediatrician and had Justin examined. Soon they both recovered. We finally settled on a Family Practice D.O. for our medical care. I needed a doctor. I was pregnant again.

The most interesting of our tales of the ER is one involving electrocution. The star of this story is Justin. It was a beautiful summer day. We were readying ourselves to go to the airport in St. Louis. Nicholas had traveled with my mother to see my brother in Canada.

The Victorian house had beautiful large windows in a bay window shape. The windows were six feet tall. They were open. A gentle breeze was causing the curtains to billow. The scene seemed so peaceful. Just a normal day filled with activities needed for our trip to St. Louis and then on to Columbia where my mother lived at the time.

There were not adequate electric outlets in the bathroom, so I was drying my hair in the living room. Justin came to help me plug my hair dryer in the receptacles behind the couch below the windows.

He crawled behind the couch and inserted the plug into the receptacle. *Ouch! Oh, OH MY GOD! Help! OUCH!!!* He screamed for what seemed an eternity as I questioned and came to his aid. He had gotten an electrical shock. It hurt. It hurt very badly. His right hand was bright red.

Even though I feared we'd miss my mother's flight, I had to take him to the ER. He continued to scream. Quickly he was attached to wires and a heart monitor. The image of your son on an exam table with wires is not one you forget. They talked seriously about the damage that can happen to the heart with electrocution. I thought about one of my stepsister's nephews who had been hit with lightening in his house and died. I was scared.

Justin continued to scream. They gave him a narcotic for pain. They gave me a prescription for a narcotic and sent us on with instructions to follow up in a few days if he wasn't any better. His heart seemed to be okay. The trip to St. Louis was longer than usual as I was worried about Justin. We continued to my mother's as planned. Justin didn't improve.

I called the clinic that had served our medical needs in Columbia. They still had our medical records. They said sure, come in. Multiple doctors examined his hand. They were puzzled and started talking about gangrene. His hand had been so damaged it might need to be amputated.

We went back home with instructions to monitor his progress and come back in two days. From all the narcotics, he was sleepy. He laid down over the air conditioning vent and fell asleep on my mother's floor.

I was worried about Justin. My mother was as well but she was also observant.

While he was sleeping on the floor, she looked at him then at me. She asked, "*what hand was he complaining about when this first happened?*" I pictured the frightening seen in the ER the first day. I thought hmm, it was the right hand. Then she asked, "*what hand is he complaining of now?*" I answered, "*the left.*"

Did it ever hurt at all? He continued to plead innocence. It had hurt. It still hurt. We knew better. Likely, he did get a shock and when he saw my reaction, it snowballed from there. But his hand was red, what caused that? Then I remembered. He had made red Kool-Aid just before he came to help me.

There were so many situations like this that space does not allow me to share them all. There was one more noteworthy tale. This one involved Elizabeth. Justin and Elizabeth had walked out the door to walk to school. Nicholas was in High School and went to school with his dad in the morning.

We gave each other kisses and well wishes for the day. They thought I would leave soon. I went to the car parked in front of the house. Catching a glimpse of them around the corner, I was suspicious. I moved the car around the other corner and quickly snuck back into the house. I watched the front of the house from the kitchen.

One of the large windows in the living room started to make noise. I hid myself. First Elizabeth climbed in, then Justin. You should have seen their faces when I came out of the kitchen and asked what they were doing. They went to school.

Between their antics, and all the drama, it is no wonder things began to go downhill fast. Life turned hellish. Things happened in those years that are hard to explain. I won't try. It was just unbelievably bad. Our family was falling apart in every way possible. What was supposed to be a place of new beginnings and respectability was turning into living hell as we awaited another May baby.

I prayed I would have a boy. Maybe if I gave my husband a son it would help. I knew he wanted a son. Just like I was desperate for a girl when Elizabeth was born, he wanted a son.

My husband was talking about going back to his home in South Asia. He was not happy with his job. He wasn't happy with much.

I was sick the whole pregnancy. I didn't gain any weight. I was six pounds lighter when I delivered than when I conceived. I was overweight so no one considered it concerning. But things were not right physically or emotionally. I continued to work throughout the pregnancy and made it until a few weeks before term. I decided to have the baby in the hospital where I worked. I also decided that I would stay in the hospital as long as I could.

Sometimes we would talk about all of us moving to South Asia. I could not do it. I had three American children that would have such a challenging time adjusting. But what would I do? I'd have six children to care for alone.

SIXTEEN

Once again, I had a May baby. This was my fourth May child. But this May child was a boy. I still didn't know if I would be raising this boy alone. There had been a date set and a ticket bought for my husband's departure. At the time I was too devastated to think rationally. In retrospect, I have some understanding of his desire. Sometimes life overwhelms you so much and you just want to run away. I'd felt that many times. And if you had a "home" to go to, all the better.

I noticed something about this beautiful boy. His eyes were not brown at birth like his sisters. They were bluish. In the iris of his right eye, there was a miniscule speck. Also, his right eye shed tears. I knew that newborns didn't cry tears.

When he would get upset and cry, the right quadrant of his forehead would get red and blotchy. I called the doctor's office about the tears. The nurse quickly dismissed me as an over-concerned new mother.

At six weeks, our son and I both went for our check-ups to the same doctor. That's one of the advantages of the Family Practice doctor. They know and treat the whole family. I was pronounced able to return to work after delivering an 8lb 13oz boy.

When the baby was examined, the doctor kept looking at his right eye. He said, "*I don't like the way his eye responds.*" Before we left, he called the only ophthalmologist in Hannibal. He was a crotchety old man about to retire. He had an office on the second floor of a building on Broadway. We were told to go immediately.

He had no nurse or receptionist. He was the only one there. He took the baby and started his examination. He had no special equipment. Just some handheld stainless-steel tools. At one point he put an instrument on his right eyeball. It was used to measure eye pressure. I watched in horror.

Dad was waiting in the car outside. Dad was entertaining our youngest daughter while I was with the doctor. She was two. I don't think he grasped the seriousness of our sons condition or my anxiety.

Our two-year-old daughter started yelling out the car window at a woman who walked past the car. She yelled, "*Why are you walking on my road?*" He thinks the story is funny, and it is. He tells it often. He makes no connection between that story and what I was dealing with in the doctor's office. When he tells the story, it reminds me of the day I was in that little dark doctor's office wondering what would happen next and I find it hard to laugh.

Interrupting my thoughts, the doctor said: "*I think your son has glaucoma. It's rare in children. He was born with it.*" He referred us to a specialist at Barnes Hospital in St. Louis. We were to be there the next morning.

My mother came to Hannibal to watch the children. She hated coming to Hannibal. There was no time to take them to her. Early the next morning we took our first of many trips to Barnes Hospital.

After an examination in the office, they admitted him to the hospital. An examination under anesthesia was scheduled for the next morning. We settled into a room in the Children's Hospital. A resident came in and took photographs of our son and his eye. The took notes and queried us repeatedly. Everyone was so serious. I still didn't know if I'd be facing other visits to a hospital as a single mother. I feared he would be blind, or perhaps worse.

With instructions to not feed him after midnight, we made our beds on the floor under his crib. We were in a large room with four other families and their children. All the cases were difficult. We politely asked about the other children and told our story to the other anxious parents. We didn't sleep. I snuck him under my breast a few times. I couldn't stand to hear him cry for food.

They came for him early the next morning. He was hungry and cranky. A few hours later, he returned with his arms in splints to prevent him from touching his eye. He had black eyes. He looked like he'd been beaten or in a car accident. He was six weeks old.

The doctor came and told us, "*Yes, it is glaucoma, but it is atypical. I'm not sure what's going on.*" After our son regained consciousness and was fed and changed, we were released with medication and a thousand questions. I asked everyone I knew to pray.

I never heard another word about going back to South Asia from my husband after that day. Love and perhaps some pity overtook him. Thankfully, he stayed. We never talked about again.

We made multiple trips to St. Louis. By the end of his first year, he had been at the hospital for examinations under anesthesia 10 times. We also made two trips to Tulsa, Oklahoma. The first trip was to take our son to City of Faith Hospital. This was a beautiful state of the art hospital that was part of Oral Roberts' healing ministry. We had a wonderful experience with the doctors and the prayer teams. The Ophthalmologist we saw mentioned some concern about his retina but there were no miracles.

The second time we went to attend healing services held by Oral and Richard Roberts. We stayed for a few days. My mother and the two youngest girls went with us. I don't remember who watched Nicholas, Justin, and Elizabeth. Likely people from the church.

We found seats and returned to those seats every time we went to Mabee Auditorium on the Oral Roberts University campus. Seated nearby was a couple with a five-year-old child in their arms. This little boy had fallen in a pool and was unconscious. There was no medical hope for this child.

We met them in the elevator one day and started talking. They told us their story and we told them ours. Then the conversation turned to wishing that Oral Roberts would have a healing line like the old days. That if maybe he or Richard laid hands on our child, they would be healed.

My husband was moved with so much compassion for that comatose child they held in their arms. He said to me, "*Joyce, why can't you pray for this boy.*" I thought, what? Yes, I believed in healing. Yes, I knew how to pray. But to pray for this child? I didn't know what to do. But I did the only thing I could do, I bowed my head and prayed that in the Name of Jesus the child would live.

I would learn more about healing as time went on. I learned that sometimes God heals and sometimes in His wisdom, He doesn't. I learned that faith could move mountains, even ridiculously tiny amounts of faith. I also learned that He tells us to ask. So often we don't even ask. I learned that lesson over a small coffin many years later.

We packed up our car the second time and left Tulsa. Our son was three months old, and I was scheduled to take that trip to St. Louise on Monday morning. The day before, a Sunday, I was in church. I asked once again for prayer. Our son was anointed with oil. The congregation prayed again for healing in Jesus' name.

As I turned to walk away an older woman from the church approached me. She told me she had been watching the 700 Club on TV. I nodded. I was skeptical but I did believe in the supernatural and miracles. I had seen too many not to believe.

This woman was a little odd so that affected my trust in what she was going to say. She shared that Pat Robertson had a "word of knowledge from the Lord" on TV the night before. He said he saw a baby. He said the baby had an eye problem and that it was a tumor behind his eye. He said that God was healing that baby. The tumor was gone in Jesus name. She said she claimed that miracle for my son.

I thanked her. I dismissed what she said. We had so many conversations with the doctor. They never mentioned a tumor. The people in Tulsa never mentioned it either. There was another baby with a tumor. I appreciated her thoughts and care, but she was wrong.

After the checking in procedures, Dr. Katz came into the room with his chief resident Dr. Barnaby. He said *"I've been trying to evaluate your son's situation. I have decided there has to be a tumor behind his eye. We have never been able to see well enough behind his eye. I am certain there is a tumor there."* I was speechless.

He continued,

"I know we've talked before about removing his right eye.

I believe we must remove it. It's close to the brain and if there is a tumor, it must come out.

If this was my child, that's what I would do, and this is my best medical advice.

We need your signature on this form for permission."

My husband had told the doctor several times that he didn't want the eye removed. He would declare to him that we believe God heals, and if you take his eye out, what will God heal? He was a firm no on removal.

My husband wasn't there. The doctor and I agreed that I would give permission and that if my husband still objected, he would talk to him. The doctor assured me that if he could get a better look, he wouldn't take the eye out. And if when my husband came, he still objected, he'd tear up the consent form.

I called everyone I could think of to pray. Suddenly that strange woman at church the day before wasn't so strange. I waited for my husband to show up. Dr. Katz came back in and talked to him. We agreed. We didn't sleep that night either. What would the morning bring?

I carried my precious baby in my arms to the door of the Operating Room. It was time to say good-bye. We kissed him. Shedding tears, I handed him to the OR nurse. I lingered until the door shut. I wondered how I was going to take care of this baby. Would I know how to deal with whatever came with having no eye? It was one thing to think of someone being blind, it was another to think of there being no eye. I knew that eventually he'd get a prosthesis, but he was a baby and wouldn't immediately have a prosthesis.

My husband and I went to the cafeteria. We bought a Danish and looked at it. Neither of us wanted to eat. We sat in silence and terror. It seemed years before we were notified that he was being taken to recovery. We went to meet him. Dr. Katz called the room.

"I don't understand it! I was sure. I was 100% sure there was a tumor. We've never been able to really see behind the eye before. Today, we could. And there is no tumor. I really don't understand it!"

We had a miracle. Next would come the announcement that he could see well out of that eye. That news hasn't come. He does have some very limited vision in that eye, but it isn't functional vision. While not a complete healing, no one will ever convince me that he wasn't healed. I am convinced he did have a tumor and because of that strange woman's faith and all the prayers that had been prayed, Jesus healed him.

Our son developed normally in every other way. He loved music. As a baby he would rock like Stevie Wonder. On one of our trips to the hospital a resident was talking to us. He had been watching the baby hold a transistor radio and sway to the music. The resident told us something that no one else had told us before.

He said, *"we were sure he would be developmentally disabled and never able to function. We assumed you would have to institutionalize him eventually. But he's normal. He is perfectly normal except he doesn't see out of one eye."*

Our days in Hannibal were about to end. I never went back to work after our son was born. My husband's contract wasn't going to be renewed at the school. The job search started again.

I designed a nice resume for him. I took it to a printer. It had to be professional and standout. I chose beige paper with brown ink for the resume. Matching stationery was designed. I sent hundreds of letters trying to find his next job. Letters with resumes went to public school systems in Missouri. Other letters went to land-grant universities for jobs in Cooperative Extension.

I had a complicated job search system. I typed all letters with carbon doubles, so we had records. That made follow-up letters or further inquiries possible. One file box was for public school systems, and it was divided between cold calling letters and responses to openings. The other file box was for Cooperative Extension jobs and divided in the same fashion. Each box had a place for rejection letters. I sat at the kitchen table for hours typing on a Brother electric typewriter we bought with credit at Sears.

We had a contingency plan. I started looking for jobs in Columbia. I had clerical skills and would be quickly employable. All eight of us would move into my mother's two bed trailer for a while.

I was so ready to leave Hannibal. The members of the family old enough to remember our experiences shutter at the mention of the word Hannibal. It was a horrible time for us.

As the result of a cold call letter to the University of Connecticut, my husband got an interview for a job with Cooperative Extension. He was successful and soon we were headed to Connecticut. Once again, I thought it would be wonderful. We would have more money and be accepted and respectable.

For many years after we left Hannibal, I would have nightmares that we moved back to 2007 Grace Street. I would wake up in a sweat, moaning, screaming, or crying. I had night terrors. My heart would race. Twenty-five years after we left Hannibal, on a trip to Missouri, we went to Hannibal to exorcise it out of my soul. I've only had one nightmare since then.

SEVENTEEN

I was so excited on that first trip to Connecticut. Growing up in Brooklyn, I was taught that Connecticut was for rich people. I knew many families who moved to Staten Island, a few who moved to Long Island, and rarely a move to New Jersey. In my childhood mind, this meant that if you moved out of Brooklyn you were rich. I would ask my mother why we didn't move, she said, "*we can't afford it.*"

But Connecticut was different. It was high-class. We stayed in Old Saybrook on the Connecticut Sound. Ocean breezes and salt air filled my soul with expectation and hope. I had lived near ocean water in Brooklyn and missed it so much in Missouri. We stayed at a Howard Johnson with a restaurant attached. Tasty food and clean rooms with gorgeous spring rhododendrons in bloom were all harbingers of good things to come.

He went for his interview with a committee. He told them in the interview that he was impressed with the hills and bluffs over the Connecticut River in Haddam. There was a majestic castle overlooking the river. I ignored the fact that there was also a place called the Devil's Hopyard nearby.

Commenting on the hills and bluffs, my husband told the interview committee that they were the perfect place for goats. I think they might have been silently amused by that comment. They selected him to be the new county agriculture agent for the University of Connecticut Cooperative Extension.

Driving our brown Ford Escort wagon back home, I sat in the front seat holding our one-year-old baby. Nicholas occupied the back seat. He was selected to come along to help with the baby. We discussed Yale as a good option for eye treatment for our baby son. The other children stayed with my mother. As we drove through Pennsylvania, everyone was asleep except the driver, my husband. This is where I learned to never to fall asleep while he drives. It was dark and lonely driving through the Turnpike in western Pennsylvania.

He missed the sign that said I-70 West. We were on our way to Pittsburgh instead of Wheeling WV. I woke up and asked if we'd left the Turnpike yet. He shrugged his shoulders and grunted. After consulting the Road Atlas, we took a secondary road to get back to the interstate. I dozed off again.

During the loneliest darkest time of night, a deer jumped out of the woods. I screamed. The baby cried. Nicholas gasped. The deer had hit the front of the car and the car hood popped open. Fortunately, only the deer was hurt. While he wired the hood back to the car in the dark, I prayed on the front seat. The car was running, so we drove on. Stopping at a Highway Patrol barracks we reported our accident and by the grace of God drove back to Missouri.

The insurance adjuster came and confirmed the car was totaled. Armed with a small check, we started to look for a new car. After multiple trips from Hannibal to St. Louis we found a beautiful middle class, suburban mom station wagon.

A fast-talking salesman worked some magic and we drove away in a white 1984 Pontiac 6000 station wagon. I love station wagons. We've had a lot of cars since then, but that car is the all-time favorite. It was like a royal carriage to me. It could comfortably seat eight people. We were a family of seven at the time, so no one was crowded. Kids often fought over who would ride backwards in what we called the "backer."

The day before we moved from Hannibal, friends came to help us load the truck. Despite all the pain and trauma, we experienced in Hannibal, we did have a few good friends. They worked so hard in the early heat of summer. The truck was loaded. We lined up on the floor to sleep for our last night at 2007 Grace Street.

The next morning some of those same friends returned to pray with us as we left for our new life in Connecticut. We planned to drive straight through but ended up sleeping at a rest stop on the Pennsylvania Turnpike. We had a cargo clamshell attached to the racks on the top of the car. It had essentials in it. Someone needed an essential. It was a child, and it wasn't essential, but we retrieved it anyway. As we resumed our trip to the promised land, I saw my clothing flying all over the Turnpike. Whoever shut the clamshell didn't close it all the way. I can still see my favorite brown jumper that served as a maternity dress for three children flying into the windshield of another car. Fortunately, it blew off quickly and no accident ensued.

We had found a townhouse to rent. Everyone fell in love with Jerry's Pizza. This was real pizza, not cardboard with sauce. The grease would drip down the sides. I instructed the kids how to fold the pizza like a New Yorker. Do not ask for a knife or fork! Authentic pizza was the food of the gods and to attack it with silverware was a sacrilege. No more Pizza

Hut or fake pizza for us. We now had the real thing. A trip to Vecchitto's on the way home meant Italian ice in a pleated white paper cup.

People moved faster and talked faster. It felt like home. It felt like Brooklyn. But it was prettier and greener. I soon found excuses to take the 2.5-hour trip into Brooklyn. I found out that nothing was the same. No one lived there anymore. But I still liked to go. I took the trip to participate in the Norwegian Constitution Day parade in Brooklyn once again. Every year at Thanksgiving I would swear that next year we'll go to the Macy's Thanksgiving Day parade. We never did.

My mother came to visit in the early fall. We picked her up at LaGuardia and took her immediately to 53rd Street to see our old home in Brooklyn. She was not as enamored with being there as I was. I presented her with flowers to welcome her back to Brooklyn. We got an Italian Ice from a vendor. We visited my cousin and took her home.

She did like being in Connecticut with us. She canceled her trip back home until the next summer. After a year in Connecticut, she planned to stay permanently. The next summer, I drove her back to Missouri. After many yard sales, sorting, and packing she officially moved away from Missouri for a life of living with her daughter in Connecticut. That enabled me to work and supplement the family income.

Connecticut was the best of everything for me. Food and people like I knew in Brooklyn, but with natural beauty surrounding us. There weren't many Norwegians but there were lots of Italians and Polish folk. We went to a church pastored by an Italian. His wife was Swedish, and she knew all about the church I grew up in, Salem Gospel Tabernacle. He and his wife graduated from the same Bible school as a previous pastor. All were spiritual markers I knew and could trust.

The first unwelcome news we got was that there wouldn't be a paycheck for two months. We had nothing. We were almost broke. Our rent was paid. We'd made it to Connecticut. But we didn't have enough to survive for two months.

I knew what to do. I found out where the welfare office was located. We had received commodity cheese in Hannibal but gone were the days of food stamps. In Hannibal they gave us 5 lbs. of cheese per person per month. We were a family of 8. That was 40 lbs. of cheese a month. I didn't relish the idea of applying for Food Stamps. I did what was necessary.

We were granted emergency Food Stamps. Because of our family size, it was a substantial amount. I planned how every penny would be spent. I stretched the Food Stamps for 3 months, not just 2. People still stared and sometime commented when I pulled out the fake money, but we had to eat.

The children were enrolled in school. They learned to say they wore sneakers not tennis shoes. I was so excited I could buy them at a store known for good brands rather than K-Mart. Their sneakers had the Nike swoosh on the side. School clothes were not hand-me-downs or from a charity.

In Connecticut there was no sales tax assessed on children's clothing or food. That was a major help. At school I asked for the list of school supplies I needed to buy. The principal gave me a blank stare. Then he informed me that in Connecticut *"we supply everything the child needs to learn."* I said, *"Even crayons?"* He said, *"Yes."*

EIGHTEEN

Nicholas didn't adjust well. He was now a teenager. I don't feel that the details of his story are mine to tell. For a short while he lived in a shelter. Later he went to Missouri to live with Allen. I still feel great sadness when I think that at such an immature age he left home. I also have feelings of guilt. I was too young and too damaged to adequately love and parent him as I should.

Oh, the dreams I had for my firstborn. As soon as Nicholas was released from the hospital after his birth, he was in church 3-4 times a week: Sunday morning, Sunday night, Wednesday night and Youth Group. I meant it when he was dedicated on Easter Sunday morning. I had given him to the Lord, and I knew God would use him.

But there was another thought I remember having shortly after he was born. "Now I finally have someone who will love me." I grew up with performance expectations. I firmly understood and believed that I was put on the earth to make my parents happy. I had failed miserably. I had destroyed my mother's reputation in her hometown of Waynesboro when I didn't want to just "hang-out" with church kids.

In addition to being unwanted, I had never found a way to overcome my mother displeasure at my existence and please her. Yet I kept trying. In my warped thinking, I now thought that this child would help fill that gap for me. I would be a better mother because I wanted this child, but only in retrospect have I realized how my thinking led to bad decisions during this tough time for Nicholas.

Several scriptures speak of sins being visited on the children in subsequent generations. Those scriptures can be hard to understand or interpret. Because of the damage my parents, particularly my mother, had experienced, she didn't know how to parent her daughter. And likewise, I passed on what I knew. Unless the power of this damage is healed, each generation will continue to make the same mistakes. I was the best parent I knew how to be, but I wasn't the parent I should have been. The same anger that my mother expressed to me and the same abandonment I felt from my father when I was 14 and 15, I visited upon Nicholas and later to Justin.

We lived in the townhouse for less than a year. We started looking for a house. My husband wanted to move to a neighboring town that had good schools and a "better" standard of living. We moved. But the house we moved to was one of the worse in the more affluent town.

We worked and worked to make the house livable. The house was a two-bedroom cape with an un-dormered attic. In this two-bedroom house would live my husband and I, my mother, and five children. The house shared a driveway with two other houses on a winding narrow street. A large hill was behind the house causing water to run under the house.

There was one bathroom. My husband, who is very skilled in car repairs, knew nothing about plumbing and construction. Yet, by reading a few books, he managed to make the only bathroom into a bath and a half. To access the bathroom "suite," you went through a single door and could choose which bathroom to use. It worked.

I painted and wallpapered. The asphalt siding was replaced with lovely yellow vinyl siding. It was like putting lipstick on a pig. The kids transferred to their new schools mid-year. As I did everywhere we've ever lived, I substitute taught in the schools. Minus Nicholas and with a huge hole in my heart, we worked at improving our lives.

We lived in that first house for several years. I was pregnant. Another daughter was on the way.

There are too many stories from Connecticut to tell. Many of them are extremely difficult. In addition to not having Nicholas with us, Justin, and Elizabeth had multiple issues. Both had treatment for their issues. Elizabeth spent her 13th birthday at Christian residential treatment. She was there for a year. We made multiple trips to Vermont to see her.

I secured an exceptional job at the Town Hall as the Coordinator of Older Adult Services. Under my leadership, I would help the opening of the Town's first Senior Center. I taught the Line Dance class. I was also the exercise instructor, and the chorus director. Eventually the budget extended to hire qualified people to do these things. I successfully applied for grants. I was emerging as a leader in this field.

I applied for a job at another Senior Center in a larger municipality. I was hired. It was my dream job. When I was first hired, I would look around in unbelief. Sometimes, because I felt so blessed with that job, I would sing to myself the song from Sound of Music: *"somewhere in my youth or childhood days, I must have done something good."* It felt good to have a respectable job. It felt great to have a place where I could excel, and I did. As my reputation grew, I was appointed as a congressional delegate to the White House Conference on Aging under the Clinton administration. I saw President Clinton so many times during those years that being able to see a president in person was no longer something special. I'd received calls for leaders across the state and had several feature articles in the *Hartford Courant*.

In one of the articles in the *Courant*, I was surrounded by medical equipment. I stood in picture surrounded by an adult commode, some wheelchairs, and walkers. The Senior Center had a lending program for durable medical supplies. We joked for weeks about Joyce with the commodes.

Another newspaper article became a test case for hundreds of social work students. The article in the Courant showed a dejected woman sitting on her bed. She said that she had been suspended indefinitely from Bingo at the Senior Center. What it didn't tell was that she had engaged in loud inappropriate behavior multiple times. Her rants included ethnic slurs. The article only told one side of the story.

The article from the *Courant* was picked up by *USA Today*. Maury Povich staff called and invited me to be guests on his show. I declined. Later, I learned that this article was discussed in Social Work classes across Connecticut. They discussed if it was ethical to suspend someone from participating in a municipally funded senior center.

The Senior Center grew. I supervised social workers, nursing/medical staff, transportation drivers, kitchen workers, and more. I administered a half a million-dollar budget. Thousands of people came to our Annual Senior Expo. Vendors and providers of senior services came for endorsements or exposure.

One night Senator Christopher Dodd was speaking at my invitation at the Senior Center. This was during the Tiananmen Square crisis. I escorted him to an undisclosed area where he could be updated on the crisis. As I stood guarding the door, I thought, wow, here I am, this scrappy girl from Brooklyn listening firsthand to history being made.

Two years after our Yankee daughter was born, I was pregnant again. This was my 8th pregnancy. I wasn't happy about it. I was getting closer and closer to 40 and thought we had enough children. While life was better in some ways, with that many children, it still was difficult. Issues with Justin and Elizabeth were escalating, and I missed Nicholas.

Working full-time in a demanding job resulted in not enough time for the children. If I had it to do over again, I wouldn't have worked so much. Nevertheless, we also needed the money.

It was Saturday of Memorial Day weekend. I was sleeping on our waterbed. I was about 15 weeks pregnant. I woke up with some cramping. I walk through the living room and kitchen, down a hallway, to get to the bathroom. My dripping blood left red footprints on the carpet.

I sat on the toilet. When I got up, I looked in the toilet. Floating in the bloody water was the fetus. I reached down and picked it up. I couldn't flush a fully formed baby down the toilet. Crying I stumbled back to the bedroom with the wet and bloody baby in my hand. It was the size of my thumb.

After some tears and a few words, we wondered what do we do now? My husband took the baby, put it in a glass, and put it in the back of the refrigerator. We went back to bed. I don't think I slept.

The next morning, I called the doctor on call. He asked, *"Did you lose the placenta?"* I said, *"yes."* I thought I had. I hadn't. Much to my surprise my body released it later that day. My husband decided to show the kids the tiny perfect baby. We never moved it around to see if we could tell the gender, we left it in the glass.

There was a small old cemetery in the town in which we lived. We drove to the cemetery. My husband got out and dug a hole. We buried the baby and cried.

I was overcome with grief and guilt. I'd known women who had miscarriages. I gave them sympathy, but it had never occurred to me how devastating the level of grief experienced by them. I would get in the car and cry for my baby. Other times I'd feel the guilt of not having wanted to be pregnant. Maybe this was punishment.

A few years later, I got involved with a woman's ministry. One of the women I met had just had a miscarriage. Two others had abortions earlier in their lives. All were dealing with both grief and guilt. They told me that they had prayed and asked Jesus to tell them what the gender of their children had been and what He had named them in Heaven. While I was all about praying and spiritual things, I did think this was odd. But I prayed and asked Jesus. He told me it was a girl and that He had named her Juliette because she was a beautiful jewel. I wasn't sure that was really God, but I knew Juliette was not a named I would have ever picked. It was a nice thought and maybe true, but I wasn't going to share this odd news with anyone.

Shortly after that, another woman started emailing me the "Catholic Saint of the day." I've never been Catholic, but I would read them. One day, I thought wow, there are so many Saints! I wondered, is there a recognized St. Juliette, and if so, what is her Saint day? There was and much to my shock, her St. day had significance.

Fourteen months after we buried the baby, I gave birth to another beautiful daughter. The Saint day was that daughter's birthday. I started thinking, maybe this isn't my imagination.

Fast forwarding to the end of this story. As we were pulling into a parking lot recently, my great-granddaughter said, "Grandma, I know a perfect name for a girl." She had been compiling names for the children she hoped to have someday.

I asked her what name she picked. She said "Juliette Joyce." She'd never heard the story of Juliette. And at first, I missed the significance of what she was saying. Quickly I remembered a Saturday morning, on that exact day, 34 years before, that I held that tiny baby in my hand. The baby that the Spirit said was a girl named Juliette. I was stunned. I had never told my husband any of this story. As I told him, I cried. I cried because of the loss, but mostly I cried because of the goodness of God. I believe someday when I see Jesus, I will also see the daughter I lost that day.

At nearly 40 years old, an amniocentesis was ordered. The baby was developing normally. It was a girl! I bought so many beautiful dresses. I could afford to buy the nicer things for this child. I knew she'd be my last, so I was extravagant. Our last child was born. A healthy beautiful girl who also was the biggest child I delivered.

A few weeks after our last daughter was born, Elizabeth, who was back from the residential treatment ministry, went on a mission trip to Venezuela. Elizabeth was 15. The night before the young missionaries were to return, at 2:30 a.m., the phone woke me up. It was the pastor.

Elizabeth had separated from the group a few days before but had returned. On their last evening out, she had disappeared again. Oddly, there seemed little concern for her. Rather there was consternation that she had disobeyed the rules.

Pastor informed me that group would get on the plane in the morning, and they hoped she'd show up. That was it. Seemingly there was little concern. The pastor prayed with me. I shared the news with my husband.

I went with a friend whose daughter was also on the trip to the airport. I prayed for a glimpse of Elizabeth. Maybe at the last minute she connected with the group and was on the plane. One by one the tired young missionaries and their leaders came to meet their waiting families. Elizabeth wasn't there. One of the leaders came and said, "We all came home. She didn't return."

As I think of it now, I feel angry. I am angry that no one seemed to feel any urgency about her situation. No one stayed to look for her. They took my minor child to a foreign country and left her there. They gave me the contact information for the pastor of the church in Venezuela and went home.

On the return trip to Connecticut, I listened to my friend's daughter talk about all the things God had done through them in Venezuela. Once home, I called the missionary pastor in Venezuela. His response was "*I have some other teams coming in and I'm busy. There isn't anything I can do.*" I don't even remember if he offered to pray for Elizabeth.

We alerted the Embassy. I couldn't go to Venezuela. The baby didn't have a passport and I was breastfeeding. We didn't have the money for anyone to go to Venezuela. The local church helped all they could. I made flyers with her picture. The youth leader and my husband prepared to go to Venezuela. But that would take several days.

For the better part of the week, I had no idea whether my daughter was dead or alive. We didn't know what to do. And again, looking back, I still get angry. A child goes missing in a foreign country, no one knows where she is, and the people who were responsible for her came home. They also never asked about her again. The church that she went to minister in, did nothing to find her.

The Embassy called. She was there. I young Venezuelan man brought her there. He had taken her home to live with him until his mother told him, "*she's American and you better take her to the Embassy.*" I know a little bit of some of the things that happened to her during that time, but I doubt I know everything as she wandered the streets of Caracas alone.

When she came home, we discovered her cornea had been burned. She was examined in the ER. I thanked God that she got home. I shudder to think of all the things that could have happened. She recovered physically. More troubles followed her.

NINETEEN

We lived in Connecticut for sixteen years. There are too many trauma stories to tell. The more trauma came, the more I kept reaching out to God. I knew God. I had known Him since a child and even though I struggled with shame, unworthiness, and guilt I wasn't going to go anywhere. Only Jesus had the answer. And maybe if I just kept sticking around…things would eventually change.

Along with my job at the Senior Center, I taught Sunday School, then Children's Church. I sang in the choir. I led the Women's Ministry. I was the Sunday School Superintendent. In my "spare" time I did the bulletin every week. I wrote the visitor letters as well as the weekly letter to those who missed church. I would take attendance every Sunday morning. The letter would include a summary of the sermon.

I functioned as church secretary and assistant pastor with no official credentials or pay. The Holy Spirit worked through me. I prayed for people, and they were healed. I saw miracles happen. I preached often. It was as if the call of God was finally manifesting. It was a call I heard as a child. I had been disqualified by a divorce but perhaps God wasn't finished with me.

As I look back, I was still trying to perform to please God. I loved the Lord so much. But I didn't understand grace. I knew the word. I understood the word. I knew all the verses to Amazing Grace, but I didn't fully believe it was for me. I could tell people it was for them. Didn't matter who they were or what they did, Jesus would love them and forgave them. His grace was for all! All except for me, I needed to perform to experience even a small measure of grace.

Elizabeth was married. She had two small children. She and her husband came to church regularly. She taught Sunday School. She was pregnant with another child. In September, on the day after my father's birthdate and a few days before her older sister, a beautiful child was born. She was named after one of her aunts. Her name was *Rachel Israel*.

Our family was living in two corporate apartments because of a house fire early the December before. We were placed in a hotel. Two days after the fire, my husband returned to his native country because his father was terribly ill. He took the younger children with him. The Christmas that followed was very lonely. My mother and I occupied one hotel suite, and the other was occupied by our two teenage daughters. Justin was married with a family of his own. Elizabeth lived with her husband and three children. Nicholas lived in Missouri with his family.

The world travelers returned early in January. I had worked with insurance to secure housing. We would be displaced for seven months. Our son who was now 13, had a large bite on his abdomen. He complained of joint pain. He stayed home from school for weeks. The day that I understood how bad it was when he called me from the bathroom. He had gone to take a bath and couldn't get out of the bathtub unassisted.

That morning we were going to take him to the ER. My pager started to light up and beep. I called the office. Marjorie, my secretary answered, *"Joyce, Elizabeth is at the hospital with her daughter. They gave me this number for you to call."* I called. Finally, Elizabeth was on the phone and in halting hushed tones, she said, *"Rachel is dead."*

Elizabeth had woken up to a dead child. At first, she thought she was just sleeping, but when she tried to dress her, in horror, she knew she was dead. The ambulance came but would not let Elizabeth ride in the ambulance.

There had been several tragic and suspicious deaths of young children in the Hartford area that winter. The police thought there was foul play. One police car took her to the hospital while the remaining police stayed at the apartment with her husband and children. It was a crime scene.

The pastor and his wife, along with the deacons, and the youth pastor all headed to be with us. The youth pastor went to the apartment. The others gathered around us and the stunned mother and dead child. Every so often, Elizabeth would say, *"If I nurse her, she'll wake up."* She'd lift her shirt to no avail.

There was a man lurking around. I noticed his presence but didn't think too much about it. Immediately after they took Rachel away for an autopsy, I learned the identity of the man. He was from Child Protective Services (CPS). He said that he was there to take the other two children until the investigation was completed.

Before I took Elizabeth from the hospital, they took a lock of her hair to test for drugs. Her husband stayed at the hospital with my husband and the pastor. He had a lock taken from his hair as well. The drug tests were negative. Despite pleadings and negotiating with the CPS social worker, the children were taken.

I'll never forget the anguish of that experience. I am a fixer by nature. I couldn't fix this. Life was unalterably and forever changed. Elizabeth took a cassette tape with worship music with her to the upstairs apartment. I understand she spent much of the evening worshiping. She said she felt closest to Rachel because she was in heaven with Jesus.

That evening when I had a moment with my own anguish. I asked God why? I didn't get an answer as to why. What I did get was an image of the pastor of the church, his wife, all the church board, my best friend, the youth pastor, and my family all standing around Elizabeth in the hospital as we committed Rachel to the Lord before they took sweet Rachel for autopsy.

Jesus spoke to me. He asked, *"Last Sunday at church, if someone came in and asked all of you if you believed that Jesus could raise the dead, you would have all shouted yes, hallelujah!"* He continued, *"Yet not one of you prayed and asked me to raise Rachel. You accepted her death."* His final comment still haunts me, *"don't ever not ask me for something again."*

Several years later that same pastor's wife had cancer. As the church family gathered around her, they prayed for strength through surgery. They prayed for the doctor's hands. They prayed for peace. They briefly mentioned healing in a very generic way. I was brought back to that experience the night Rachel died. I asked if I could pray. I prayed with faith and boldness asking God to heal her in the Name of Jesus. She did well and recovered. God was healing her. Since then, I have never hesitated to pray and ask Jesus to heal in His name. I've seen a few miracles and I've also seen God walk with people as they breathe their last. All healing comes from God and the ultimate healing is when He takes His beloved child home to be with Him.

We were all numb. Elizabeth and her husband stayed with us in the apartments. We didn't know where the children were or when they would come back. We started plans for a funeral. In between we took our son to the ER. No one seemed to know what was wrong with him. On one visit, he was isolated and so were we, meningitis was feared. Tests came back negative.

We bought a small white coffin and a burial plot. On the day of the funeral, a coffin replaced the communion table in the front of the church. The church was filling up. But no sign of Elizabeth's other children.

Our church family came with food. Our children were there except the one who couldn't walk and for whom we had no answers. I went to stand in front of this precious granddaughter dressed in the same Winnie the

Pooh sleeper she was dressed in the previous Sunday. I wondered if it was too late to pray for resurrection.

I had gone to the Christian Bookstore to get folders for the funeral bulletin. I chose one appropriate for a baby dedication. It quoted 1 Samuel 1:27, *For this child I have prayed…* They don't make funeral bulletin covers for a 4.5-month-old infant.

As we gathered at the church, we continued to look at the door. There they were. The state had released custody of the two children, and they were there for the funeral. It was such a joy to see them running down the aisle. They clung to their mother. I know the younger of the two has no memories of this experience, but her older brother does. His first-born daughter is named for his sister who died too soon.

I got up to sing the old hymn, "*Savior Like A Shepherd Lead Us.*" That song had special meaning. We sang the *Cares Chorus*. Elizabeth had learned it as a child when she had her *Psalty* Praise Cassettes and Bible Cover. The Cares Chorus reminded us to *"cast all our cares on Jesus."*

I was surprised that Elizabeth also wanted us to sing, "*It Is Well With My Soul.*" We read the 23rd Psalm in English and Spanish. Personally composed poems about this precious girl were read and lots of tears were shed. A woman I knew from work said afterwards how surprised she was that we talked so much about Jesus.

After the funeral we drove to the cemetery. It was so bitterly cold. It was February in New England; we were glad there was no snow. The ground had been opened and she was placed in her final resting place. We couldn't afford a marker for her tiny grave. On what would have been her 18th birthday, I finally was able to buy a marker for her grave. It was important for her to have a marker. I wanted the world to know that she existed. She was real. And she was deeply loved.

We returned to the church fellowship hall for food. Our church family fed our bodies and our souls. For the first time, I saw the faint glimpse of a smile on Elizabeth's face. I had hoped she would heal and that she would continue reaching out to Jesus.

Within a year she had spiraled down into alcoholism as self-medication. Her husband had the children and eventually moved them away. For years, those children were lost to us.

Our son's issue still had to be resolved. I took him to our regular pediatrician. I had Rheumatic Fever as a child, and this was beginning to look the same. But no one had that disease or thought about it anymore. I asked Dr. Nelson to do the appropriate blood work. He thought it unnecessary. He and I had locked horns many times and he knew I was often correct. He ran the blood work.

I was correct. A heart specialist was contacted, and our son spent several days in the hospital and never returned to eighth grade. A homebound tutor met his education needs. He returned to middle school to participate in his graduation ceremony. He could walk. He was stronger. And would go off to High School.

What a year that was. Let me recap. In December, we had the fire. My husband took our three youngest children to his native country without me over Christmas. In February we buried a granddaughter. In February, our son was in the hospital with Rheumatic Fever. In April, my husband took another trip to be with his father. We continued to live in two apartments. I worked full-time.

In May, everything where I worked began to crumble. I had such a wonderful career. I was known everywhere for excellence in my field. I was in the newspaper regularly. Every day at lunch I would go with a close friend and colleague to the church to pray for revival.

Praying is dangerous. The forces of this world do not like the people of God praying. Early one morning I was summoned to the Town Manager who was my immediate boss. Someone had made accusations of impropriety, financial impropriety. The Town Attorney sat with my boss as they told me about the accusation. Of course, they had to investigate. I would be under a cloud of suspicion for a long time. Yet, I was also expected to do my job.

Not terribly surprisingly, I was able to do my job. May is Older American's Month and if you oversee senior services for a municipality, it is important. We had our annual volunteer recognition, our Senior Expo, and transportation recognition that month. Every week that month contained a huge event.

The accusations continued. There never was any evidence of wrongdoing. I had not stolen any money or done anything wrong. I soon realized I needed an attorney. The attorney proved to be a waste of money.

When the final report was produced, it was decided that because my children had used the work copy machine, I needed to be suspended for two weeks without pay. They had used it. They would come and help at the Senior Center. They made work copies. The attorney said it was a good deal. It wasn't.

About the same time, I had some other devastating news. My marriage was about to crumble and shatter in ten thousand pieces. I can't tell the story. It is still too painful to even think about. I literally stopped functioning.

I took a few days off which eventually lasted many months. I refused to eat. I was able to cook meals and bake cookies, but not much else. I started seeing a therapist. What came to the surface during my therapy sessions was not what I expected. And it wasn't what I went there to discuss.

After I was molested in Brooklyn at 8 years old, all I remembered was that Mr. Thompsen had asked me to kiss him on the mouth. I was never allowed to kiss my father on the mouth, only the cheek. I was told that type of kissing was not appropriate. I remembered the police coming to school, trying to identify Thompsen, and later the decoy operation outside the church. This was all I remembered.

I went from leading everything in the church to being unable to sit through a service. No hands were raised in praise. No sermons preached. No ministry of any kind. Nevertheless, I continued attending church. My body was there, but I couldn't function or participate. While other's praised God I sat. Sometimes people would come and try to pray for me. Some even tried to raise my hands up. I just stood there, numb.

About halfway through the sermon, I'd get up, go to the back of the church, and sit on the floor with my head covered. I wasn't praying. I was in the sackcloth and ashes of complete misery. My amazing church family loved me enough to let me do whatever I needed to do without criticism. It is often best to not try to fix someone. Let Jesus do the fixing.

You may ask, why did you go? The same reason I had always gone and kept going, where else would I go? Only Jesus could help me.

I asked a therapist once if what I experienced during those months of severe depression could have been what is commonly called a "nervous breakdown." I found that term vague and it certainly wasn't clinical. She responded *"yes, that is what a nervous breakdown looks like."*

During this time, I met with the pastor in his office. This was not the first Italian pastor that served when we first moved to Connecticut. But he was an Italian pastor.

I said, *"I can't hold on to the rope anymore. I've tied the proverbial knot at the end. But I just can't hold on."*

He responded, *"no you can't, you are in a freefall, and you think you're going to hit the bottom and die."* The truth was I wanted to die. Suicide was constantly on my mind. I was totally convinced that even my children would be better off without me.

He continued to prophesy about the freefall. He said, I would fall to the bottom. But I would not die. Jesus would be on the bottom with open arms to catch me. He was right. That catch took a long time and led me through a difficult journey.

One Saturday morning while still in bed, our youngest daughter came into the room. She was still young. Something was said and I heard myself say, "lick it like a lollipop." Instantly, I was nauseous. I had been having trouble with nausea for a while. And I also routinely spit out food to keep losing weight. Even though I was past the age of an anorexia diagnosis, my doctor insisted I was suffering from that condition and saw me every week to weigh me.

I started having flashbacks about Mr. Thompsen. I would talk about it to the therapist. I was deteriorating physically and emotionally. I thought about suicide all the time, just like I had as a child.

The therapist said, *"it's time. We must explore exactly what happened to you."* I struggled. I had never considered repressive memories. My memories were buried deep. Could I trust what I remembered? My husband was consulted. He would come for a session that would take as long as it must. It took several hours.

The day came for this marathon session. My husband was in the other room available to take me home. No one knew what exactly would happen or whether I would be able to function in any capacity. Slowly, with great pain, I recalled every minute of that encounter with Mr. Thompsen. At one point, I almost passed out. The therapist said after he almost call for an ambulance during this session. It was excruciatingly painful. I was physically sick. I threw up on the couch as I remembered throwing up on Mr. Thompsen's shoe.

Honestly, I am not sure if there was more to the story of Mr. Thompsen. Part of me still wonders if I ever went to his house. I wonder if he did other things to me or if what I remember happened many times. I don't know. I probably will never know. I do know the thought of more doesn't haunt me. I do know that slowly by the grace of God I have experienced healing.

I had heard other women say that they wondered where Jesus was when they were molested or abused. I didn't feel that way at first. Eventually I did. These same people told me to pray and ask. Several reported that much to their shock when the answers they got were compared they found they all heard the same thing. However, they never shared what they were told.

I finally felt the anguish of O God, where were you? That is different than why. I understand why. Sin is in the world. People do sinful horrible things. It happens. I didn't need to know why. But I did want to know where Jesus was that chilly day in the doorway on 53rd Street in Brooklyn.

He told me. I thought it was an interesting answer but of course, I wasn't sure I heard right. And I thought, oh there goes my imagination. What He told me was, *I was standing right there, I was weeping and praying for your ultimate healing.* The Bible tells us that Jesus is in heaven interceding for us (Romans 8:34). Even though I had many doubts and questions, I just took that as the only answer I was going to get. Honestly, I wasn't sure how comforting it really was to know that.

Maybe a year or so later when the depression had lifted some I was at a woman's retreat. Those are glorious events. Good times, great fellowship, tasty food, and lots of Jesus fills you with energy to go back home to kids, husband, dishes, and work. I listened to a woman I knew well. I knew she had been molested as a child. I knew she had been told where Jesus was when this happened to her. I also knew she never shared it publicly.

She told her story of abuse. She told she wanted to know where Jesus was at the time. Then, for some reason, that day, she told us where He was when she was being molested. He told her the exact same thing He told me.

I wept so much that day. I stayed in the meeting room long after the others left for supper. The speaker came and prayed with me. Another woman held me close and rocked me like a baby in her arms.

I left my dream job. Got another job and was later fired from that one. I took a huge pay cut. But I started getting stronger in the Lord. I thought I had survived the "dark night of the soul." It felt like Jesus had caught me.

I was functional. Another move was around the corner. Depression continued to plague me from time to time. I always had an emergency stash of enough pills to take my life. But I was better.

My husband was offered a job in Tennessee. We decided to move. Unfortunately, this move scattered our family in ways we still find hard. To see our children, we travel in several directions. Getting all the children together in one place happens only very rarely.

TWENTY

I've just scratched the surface of my life. It's been an extraordinarily complex life. It's been a difficult life. It has been plagued with bountiful sorrow and blessed with much love. The marriage no one thought would work has extended over 46 years. By the grace of God, we hope to plan for a 50-year anniversary spectacular. Over the years we've wondered what the size of our family would be at this jubilee. If it were today there would be our eight children, several spouses, 19 grandchildren with a growing number of spouses, and 15 great grandchildren. Maybe before the Jubilee Extravaganza, there will be more to come. We are raising out oldest great-grand. She is our delight and joy. I pray to live long enough to see her children.

We have had more than our share of pain. In the last few years, we have buried two grandsons in their 20s. One left three beautiful children behind. We also buried a great granddaughter, Elizabeth's granddaughter. She died at the age her aunt Rachel died so many years before. The circumstances were very strangely similar. We have three grandchildren whose whereabouts are unknown at this point.

We have had multiple graduations and weddings. We are viewed as respectable now. I think we've reached middle class. We live in a beautiful small town in Tennessee. We can afford to go on vacations and travel to see our scattered family. We just don't see them often enough.

The most pivotal moment of my life was the day Elizabeth was born. The day I thought my world would end Jesus gave me strength to turn in another direction. Jesus saved my life, and He gave me grace and ability to get an education. It's never too late for an education.

I finished my bachelor's degree in 1978. There was no ceremony. There was no cap and gown. I never got to go back to finish a graduate degree. That is, until I did.

I strongly heard a call to ministry as a child. I would be a missionary, or a pastor's wife. I did street evangelism when I was 10. I carried my Bible to school. Yes, I was trying to ease the guilt and shame I felt but it was also a desire to be used by God.

I started hearing the voice of God saying, *"I'm not done with you."* I would argue, *"no I'm disqualified."* That's what the church said. You are divorced and remarried. And of course, I am a woman. That alone disqualifies me in the eyes of some without any other things added to it.

Once again, I clearly heard Jesus speak to me. He said, *"I knew you are a woman when I called you. And I know you are divorced and I'm calling you. I know who you are married to, and I'm still calling you. I know all the reasons you think you are disqualified and I'm still here calling you."* Slowly I kept stepping further out into the deeper waters.

Shortly after moving to Tennessee, I was ordained by a small ministerial fellowship in Alabama. I also started pursing ordination with the denomination I had been with all my adult life, The Assemblies of God. I had the backing of the individual who would eventually hold a high ranking in the denomination. The Lord said no, and I withdrew my interest.

I started a small church on Music Row in Nashville. Meeting at a coffee shop, a small group of us would worship, pray, and preach the gospel. The building is now a Chuy's Restaurant, and we often go to eat there. I like to sit in the booth in the spot where I would stand to preach.

This coffee shop closed so I moved on. I felt a call to go back to school. I pursued acceptance at Vanderbilt University. I got it with a 50% scholarship. I turned down their acceptance letter. It was still very expensive. Plus, theologically I wasn't a good fit. I looked at Trevecca Nazarene University. A very shortened application led to acceptance in a few days. I would start classes immediately.

I loved studying. I love the word of God and learned to read Hebrew. Not bad for an almost senior citizen. I took every class in the Old Testament I could. While going to school we also opened a coffee shop near where we lived. In the coffee shop I planted a church called *The Well*. We didn't last long but we touched a lot of lives in our brief time of ministry.

In December of 2008 I completed a Master of Arts in Biblical Studies at Trevecca Nazarene University. I had straight A's. This time I would walk in the May graduation. I finally had a graduation. Elizabeth who was doing well and her 3-year-old daughter were there along with my husband and two of our younger children. I was so happy to have a cap on my head and a gown with a master's degree hood.

The music started and the faculty streamed across the lawn. It rained a little. When it was my turn to walk across the stage, I beamed. I had finally achieved the graduate degree. Dr. Boone, President of Trevecca met me smiling. He'd taught my preaching classes. He understood my joy.

I went on to study at Sioux Falls Seminary. In an odd twist to our lives, my husband took a job in South Dakota for three years. At SFS I attempted to cobble together the credits needed for a Master of Divinity degree. Too late I discovered that this was necessary for admission to a Doctor of Divinity program. I had set my goal remarkably high.

Depression reared its head again while in South Dakota. The northern plains can be a crucible. Many people have gone to that part of the country and lost their minds or found them. I read the Norwegian classic, *Giants in the Earth*. The setting was a few miles from where we lived in South Dakota. The mother of the story lost her mind. I thought I would lose my mind there as well.

It was my husband's turn to have his dream job. We lived in a small apartment. He was excited every day to use his gifts to benefit the people of South Dakota. I on the other hand was thinking increasingly about my bottle of pills.

One night, when things were particularly bad, after a loud disagreement with my husband, I went in the bathroom screaming, "*I am doing it now.*" I meant it. I had the bottle of pills in my hand. He came to the locked bathroom door.

I stood there, shaking. It was time. I was sure there was no other way out. I couldn't live with this deep internal pain anymore. At that moment, by the grace of God I took the bottle and threw it on the floor. I couldn't do it. The grace of God stopped me. I was angry I spilled the pills instead of taking them. Why couldn't I do it?

I picked up the scattered pills. They were precious. I still might need them. It was a very frigid winter night when I grabbed a coat and my keys and went to the car. It was near midnight. I drove south thinking I'd go to Tennessee. Then I drove north, thinking maybe I'd get a hotel room and start off in the morning. I could barely see the road for the snow haze and my tears. My husband started calling on the cell phone.

He had called the police. Now I really needed to find a way to get off the road. I didn't want to be found by the police. I was angry that he called the police.

The police called on the phone. I tried to respond. They told me to go home. After several phone calls I relented. It was cold and I didn't want to go to a hotel. I had the pills with me, and I wasn't sure I'd live to morning.

I felt trapped, so I went back to the apartment. I cried all night. The police came with a social worker who said she would be calling my therapist and if I didn't contact her in the morning, she'd be back to take me to the hospital.

As odd as this sounds, the next morning I went to class at Sioux Falls Seminary. I had arranged to see the therapist and her office was on the bottom floor of the Seminary. No one ever told me to give them my pills. I don't know if I would have. They were my security blanket.

Taking classes and being in therapy helped fill my time. It gave me a measure of usefulness and purpose. No one at the time knew anything of the hell I was going through. Someone asked me one time, *What does God have for you in the storehouses of snow?* It was a reference to Job 38:22. It was very fitting. I started writing a blog of the same name.

While I learned a lot at SFS and encountered many godly professors I was becoming increasingly academic. Also, some professors had no use for women preachers. And I was too old in their estimation for pursuing much of anything.

I shifted again. I returned to Trevecca Nazarene University to complete a Doctor of Education degree. I did research in community, social networking, and adult discipleship from 2012-2013. I was the odd duck in that pond, and no one could see the research amounting to anything. And then came covid and suddenly, I was called a digital prophet.

I marched in a second graduation ceremony, this time in a gym on Trevecca's campus because of rain. This time I didn't have a cap and gown, I wore a doctoral tam on my head, and a Trevecca purple gown with chevrons indicating that I had the title, Doctor. Around my neck was a large and uncomfortable academic hood.

I began to pursue ordination in the United Methodist Church. It was a door partially open to me. I never would be ordained but I served as a License Local Pastor for ten years at a small rural church near Nashville.

Currently, I am ordained by the new expression of Wesleyan Methodist Holiness theology, the Global Methodist Church. I am waiting for what God has for me in ministry. The only thing I know is I must write my story.

Earlier this year, I attended a women's retreat. I knew no one. I only went to hear a 97-year-old fiery woman preacher. I watched in awe how this tiny woman stood preaching through the power of the Holy Spirit for 45 minutes. The next morning, she got up and did it again. As well over a thousand woman gathered around the front for one last time of anointed praise, worship, and prayer I joined them. I felt I had come home. It was exuberant and holy worship.

As I was praying a gentle hand touch my shoulder. Then another would come. Gentle strangers came to pray for me. As I was worshiping with my hands upraised, yet another person came to pray with me. She wrapped her arms around my waist. It felt different. It felt like a mother hugging her daughter. Who was this?

I peeked to see; it was the 97-year-old preacher. Whatever happened that day was momentous. The power of God poured healing all over me and through me. I know I am healed of childhood trauma. A mother came and hugged me like my mother couldn't when I was young.

I am healed of never being wanted. I am healed of being rejected so many times; I am healed of the rejection of my mother. Months later I still feel the impact of those prayers and that hug. I am finding truth in the scripture that says, *the joy of the Lord is your strength* (Nehemiah 8:10).

My story is not a fairy tale. But it has a happy ending. I am so thankful for the work of God in my life. And when I die, I will "live happily ever after" with Jesus. Life will continue to be like twin rivers, one named joy and the other sorrow. Joy and sorrow are twin rivers running through the terrain of life. I know there is more joy and more sorrow yet to come.

> *Through many dangers toils and snares,*
> *I have already come.*
> *Tis grace hath brought me save thus far.*
> *And grace will lead me home.*

Jesus gave me strength to overcome all the difficult challenges and experiences I've endured. Had He not helped me that day by the hospital window. If He hadn't said, "You don't know if you don't try," where would I be? I don't know. But I know His grace is sufficient. His strength is made perfect in my weakness. And I know He can do that for you.

Printed in the USA
CPSIA information can be obtained
at www.ICGtesting.com
JSHW012057101223
53348JS00001B/2